# GREEN LANE FARM

*Dedicated to*

# OLD NART
## AND
# ALL THE MEN ON THE LAND

How can he get wisdom that holdeth the plough . . . and whose talk is of bullocks? . . . he giveth his mind to make furrows . . . so every carpenter . . . the smith also sitting by his anvil . . . so doth the potter . . . all these trust to their hands, and every one is wise in his work . . . without these cannot a city be inhabited. . . .

They shall not be sought for in public counsel nor sit high in the congregation. . . .

But they will maintain the state of the world and all their desire is in the work of their craft.

ECCLESIASTICUS 38: 25–34

# GREEN LANE FARM

## B. A. STEWARD

Illustrated by
BRIAN WALKER

FARMING PRESS LTD
Wharfedale Road, Ipswich, Suffolk IP1 4LG

*First published 1982*

ISBN 0 85236 128 9

Printed in Great Britain by
Redwood Burn Limited, Trowbridge, Wiltshire.

# AUTHOR'S NOTE

*When Sam on Green Lane Farm threw the last root of my 1940 sugarbeet harvest into the lorry he said, as was his habit on this annual occasion—'That's the one we've been looking for!'*

*Lifting these roots out of the clay had been a heavy job but there was sugar in it or, as my neighbour Old Ben aptly described it, 'a little sugar for the bird', which meant something for himself. So far as I was concerned there was more than I expected. For on the last day of that year the postman cycled down the green lane to bring me a letter from London.*

*It told me that a story I had sent on the impulse of the moment to the* Daily Herald *in Long Acre—'Well, the Sugar's In'—would appear in that paper the next day.*

*Thus, quite by chance, my sugar harvest over, a longer and more exacting job began. I had to put my hand to the 'plough in Long Acre'.*

*For I wrote another story the next week, and the next, and went on doing it for twenty years. It took the form of a weekly* Country Diary *which told a simple tale of country folk, to a readership mainly of townspeople.*

*It was the story of a farm family. In it were Old Nart,*

*Sam, Mary the land-girl, the boy George, Old Ben on the next farm, Herbert my town friend, Mr Britten the schoolmaster, and other cronies met with at the Shepherd & Dog and elsewhere.*

*A farm family which included my Suffolk horses Honey, Captain, Princess and Old Don, the old cows Buttercup and Judy, Susan the Sow, my dogs Scruffy and George and Sally. Not to forget Helen the speckled hen, the turkeys, geese and ducks, and the twenty-odd cats and kittens that lived in the barn but never failed to turn up in the cowhouse at milking time.*

*In these pages I hope they all come back to life again, and with them the old-fashioned farming of the forties which, with all its faults and lack of modern ideas and machines, yet contrived to put back into the land more than it took out, to make each farm a better farm, and to produce—under natural conditions that alone are capable of producing it—good food, the only food really worth eating.*

*In brief, the gospel according to Old Nart.*

*He and Sam and their generation have passed away, but much of what they argued about, not only in the Shepherd & Dog but also in barn and field and stackyard and stable, at haytime and harvest, still holds good today.*

Felixstowe                                    *B. A. Steward*
July, 1982

# OCTOBER

*'Rook alone, rain soon,' warned Old Nart, looking up at a solitary bird in the sky. It meant we had to get a move on.*

*Sowing the* Holdfast *wheat on the ploughed-up old meadow was a great event on the farm. It had not happened for more than a century. It would be talked about for years to come. Like feeding the five thousand, a war-time miracle, using this poor grass, and countless other old meadows like it, to give us our daily bread, just at the time when food was most needed.*

*The sun of St Luke's Little Summer shone on the hips and haws in the hedges, and on the brown coats of the Suffolk horses harnessed in the drill. The year was 1942.*

# Sunshine sowing

HONEY, MY pedigree Suffolk mare, is in one of her moods today. But this is a great occasion. On the old meadow we are sowing *our daily bread*.

Fat sacks of seed lie sprawled along the brow of the ditch on one side of the field. Sam, with the Suffolk horses, Princess and Old Don, helped by the boy George behind the new combine-drill, are doing the sowing. As this is a special occasion, Old Nart has also come along to take charge of Honey and the old horse Captain and harrow-in the seed behind the drill. It is just like Honey to choose such a day to get into one of her tantrums, to froth at the mouth, rear up on her hind legs, walk with her head in the air and her ears back, and do a step-dance over the clogs like a hackney at a show. She is already breathing like a steam-engine, and her chestnut coat is black with sweat.

But we forgive her. Indeed we would forgive her anything.

Buying her at a farm sale for fifty pounds seven years ago was one of the best investments I have ever made in all my farming career. In fewer words Sam called it 'a good move'. For since then she has bred two sons and three daughters, and four of them have already brought credit to her in show and sale-ring, while the fifth now trots round the meadow and is destined one day, we hope, to be queen of the farm.

Which merely underlines what Old Nart was arguing about in the Shepherd & Dog the other day, that not only do they crush the land down and pull it up in unworkable chunks but Tractors Don't Breed.

☆

PATIENCE then. Old Captain sets a good example. Taking no notice of the mare's prancing except to give her a playful bite now and again when they turn on the headlands, he seems to dismiss it all with a shrug and to say, 'There, on the rampage again! Well, you can't account for them. And what would you expect after six months' holiday with her foal on the meadow?'

So, with the young mare half-trotting beside him, he sets out on another journey down the field, harrowing-in the wheat, moving surely and steadily in an unhurried plod that will finish the job and last out the day. It is good to see this kind seed-bed (so different from the usual 'sowing in the slop' of wheat seeding) with the sun of St Luke's Little Summer in early October shining down, and to think that we are sowing seed that, now that food is so important, may bless us with yet another bountiful harvest. And to glance at Old Nart, when the sky is darkening, and the sowing finished, seeing him still toiling behind his ill-matched pair, covering the seed with the harrows.

9

Better still, when the harrowing is done, and the big white owl hovers silently over the stable, to watch him unharnessing Honey, patting her neck and whispering to her the farming wisdom of the ages. The words of an ancient philosophy for horses—*and for men.*

'You don't want to get yourself worried and upset about doin' a little work a-harrowin' the wheat,' he tells her. 'That'll last a lot longer than you will.'

# Smiling through

IN EARLY October, while some roses remain in the garden and the last golden leaves still cling to the chestnut tree, we are thankful for any reminder of summer. The sunshine of the last few days, for example.

It is no doubt true, as Old Nart says, that we shall pay for it later on. But in the meantime we can make good use of it and get some of the sugarbeet 'put paid to' without having to work up to our waists in mud.

Yet even when days are dark and when there's what Sam calls 'a rare old horry frost' in the morning, there are, in farming as in other walks of life, consolations and reminders of sunnier days. They are welcome. Like the baled straw that brings back memories of ripening wheatfields whenever we litter it round the bacon pigs in their yard, they help us to forget the wintry days ahead.

☆

ONE such glimpse came to Sam by chance this morning just after we had watched, with thankfulness in our hearts, the mechanical muck-spreader come down the lane. It opened Old Nart's eyes. It roared over the big black heaps of muck dotted in rows all over the barley stubble, scattered them like chaff and did a week's work in a few hours.

Under the impact of its iron spinner, each heap in turn exploded like a shell and its black fragments sang like shrapnel in the air. It made the slow old ritual of the muck fork seem as dead as the dodo.

'That's the highest yet,' said Sam, as he watched a larger lump than usual soar skywards, describe an arc over his head, and then fall to earth with a bump at his feet.

☆

THERE it stayed, but only for a moment. While Sam stood staring at it, unable to believe his eyes, it suddenly came to life, and streaked away to a nearby hole in the hedge, just as he bent down to grab it.

It took Sam quite a long time to convince us when he told the story in the stable afterwards. 'Yes, it was that same old black rabbit,' he insisted. 'The big one—the one that got away when we cut the barley in that field this harvest.'

Outside the night was pitch dark and the wind was rising and there was a nip of frost in the air.

But the trifling episode of the black rabbit had taken us all back to a day of blazing sun and blue sky, and a smile as bright as a memory of harvest shone on Sam's face.

# Old Ben is in the red

AT THIS time of year many a small farmer like myself (harvest over but cash not yet to hand) is more likely to be in the red than in clover. But you can trust my neighbour Old Ben to make the best of both worlds by being in red clover.

I must explain. To be in red clover is to have some of this precious seed when it is wanted. To borrow an adjective (about the only thing I ever could borrow from Old Nart), this is one of the 'haz'able' crops. Whenever I have plenty

11

of it there is no demand and it might as well be ploughed in, but in other years, especially when Old Ben has a good crop, it makes big money.

☆

THIS is one of the big-money years, it seems. So when I saw Old Ben entering the corn exchange, hugging to himself a little round bag, I guessed it was not of sovereigns, but of red clover seed.

I walked over to his farm the previous day. The combine-harvester was then dealing with the crop. Where not long ago the bees hummed over a six-acre carpet of crimson blooms, the heads and straw of the clover were now dead and brown and gathered into rows from which the combine conjured dust and stalks and bushels of tiny yellow and purple seed.

As usual, everybody said it was a lovely sample. 'Worth at least £7 a bushel,' declared Walter, Ben's right-hand man.

No doubt Ben had this favourable verdict in mind when he tackled the merchants in the hall. 'What have you got this week?' asks one of them, looking down from the stand.

'Red clover,' says Ben, offering his bag. 'How much do you ask for it?' queries the merchant, hunting for a magnifying glass. Ben hesitates. 'What'll you give me?' he says.

The man on the stand shakes his head. 'I can't be buyer and seller as well,' says he.

The fact is that neither knows what the price of red clover seed is, yet. Then the merchant opens Ben's bag, stares for a moment, and laughs. 'Dear me, so this is what you grow on your farm!'

He spreads it out on the palm of his hand. It is Ben's turn to stare. The sample is of charlock seed, the yellow-flowered weed he has always pretended to innocent townie visitors was a lovely crop of mustard for the sheep. But what a let-down for Old Ben.

Naturally he blamed his right-hand man, Walter, for giving him a sample of weed seeds by mistake.

# Farmer's folly

WHEN MY neighbour Old Ben who sometimes buys bullocks for me sends in his bill he adds his commission to the price in a separate item, which he calls 'a little sugar for the bird'.

It is, in more than one sense, a touching phrase, and I am reminded of it whenever I see, as I did the other day, my first load of sugarbeet leave the farm. For this, you see, whatever the trials associated with it, is a cash crop. The cash refers not only to what we get for it, but also to what it costs us to get it.

But as every lorry-load of seven tons of beet represents about a ton of white sugar, there should be some for the bird. As Sam says, there's no taste in nothing.

☆

PICTURE the scene. The yellow leaves litter the lane. The load of roots looking like big bloated parsnips is piled up and netted on the lorry, ready to depart. Part of a big heap of the roots still remains on the grass verge. It is a familiar scene, and nothing seems to have changed from previous years, except that Sam is smiling.

You may wonder why. Well, this year, with the grain harvest finished in record time, we have been able to make an early start with the beet.

The idea was to steal a march on the mud. The sun shone a blessing on us. The sugarbeet were clean; the earth was firm and dry under our feet, and we could afford to smile.

We congratulated each other on this unexpected good fortune.

*That is about the most foolish thing you can ever do in farming.*

13

As Old Nart said sadly when the huntsman (who used to give him sixpence once a year for holding his horse) broke his neck—'There, there, whenever anybody comes along an' does me a bit o' good, something happens to 'em!'

☆

IT was just as sad for us. Just when it was doing us some good, something happened to the weather. It entered on a new phase—the sack and bag phase.

This morning, when I saw Sam and Old Nart trudging out into the field with sack aprons on, sacks round their shoulders, and a bag advertising pig meal round each leg, I knew the worst.

Sugarbeetin' in real earnest had started again—harvesting your sugar, out of the mud.

Yes, it was pleasing to see that first load of sugarbeet leave the lane. It will be even more pleasing to see the last.

In all the farm calendar this is the most disagreeable job we have to tackle, the hardest for horses and men.

I remember a village meeting at which a political candidate was introduced as, 'the man who gave us a new crop, the sugarbeet,' and the fierce growl this aroused from farm workers at the back of the hall. 'We've been waiting to meet him for a long time,' said Sam.

Thank heavens when it's all over. And next year?

Well, I suppose we shall grow twice as many. For every ton, you see, provides the war-time sugar ration for thirteen people for a year.

# The 'butcher cut'

BOB THE butcher—that's his job most days—gives me a warm welcome. 'Come in out of the cold,' he shouts, indicating a seat on a long form which already has several occupants.

'And here's the local to read while you're waiting.' He hands me the *Snoring Express*.

This hut of his is crowded. It represents one of our most cherished amenities—the village hairdressing saloon.

Where in town can you just walk up a garden path and get a high-class haircut for sixpence at any time on a Saturday afternoon or a Sunday morning?

☆

AND such a homely welcome? The saloon is equipped with a high-back chair, above which hangs a string bag of Bob's onions. It is lighted by an oil lamp, on which Bob occasionally warms his clippers for the comfort of his clients.

All round us hang the tools of his other trade. Happily, not for present use.

The charge is modest enough: we save threepence by reading right through the local while we wait, and a cup of tea and a biscuit are added to the bargain.

'Long or short, sir?' he asks politely when my turn comes. I have first been dressed in one of his wife's pinafores.

He keeps talking as he cuts my hair. As a final touch, I am given the once-over with a comb dipped in his special hair oil.

☆

NOT all his rivals reach this high standard. The story is told that in the next village a distinguished visitor from town was referred to the blacksmith for a shave and was shocked when that mighty man spat on his brush before lathering his customer.

'Do you always do that?' the latter protested. 'Oh no, certainly not,' said the smith. 'When it's local lads I just spit on their faces.'

'NEXT, please,' shouts Bob, flourishing a razor as if beckoning another lamb to the slaughter.

Bless me if it isn't Old Nart, here for a trim or a shave, and not before time; he certainly needs it.

# A-milking they won't go

THE LIGHT of the hurricane lantern throws queer shadows over the mud of the yard when Sam and I walk by night to see whether the strawberry roan heifer has started to calve.

We view it with mixed feelings. If she does not calve we shall have no milk. If she does, who is going to milk her? This is one example of the difference between theory and practice in farming. In theory, how nice to have 'a cow for the house', and get all the milk, cream, butter and cheese you want for next to nothing.

You know the old rhyme:

> *The friendly cow, all red and white,*
> *I love with all my heart:*
> *She gives me cream with all her might,*
> *To eat with apple tart.*

Nothing could be simpler and more delightful.

☆

IN practice, it works as follows.

Sam has a quiet word with Old Nart. Yes, he'll do anything to help, any job on the farm—except milking.

'What about you, George?' The answer comes promptly: 'I'm no *cow* man.'

'Any volunteers? Don't all speak at once.' You might as well ask for a lion-tamer. Nobody knows anything whatever about cows.

It is not until you are sitting comfortably in the Shepherd & Dog, talking to the blacksmith and the baker, that you learn that everybody you have approached, from Old Nart to the boy George, has done work as a cowman at some time or other, and knows all about it. Indeed they know too much. They know, for example, that old Buttercup and any other cow or heifer, when calved, has to be milked twice a day every day, Sundays and Christmas Day and all the bank holidays as well.

☆

MEANTIME the problem remains with us; Sam leads the way with his lantern and we splash through the mud and slide in and out of the ruts made by the carts taking the muck out to the fields. We finally arrive at the cowhouse.

Good heavens, the strawberry roan heifer has calved at last. How lovely—more milk, more cream, more golden butter. What a blessing, what a treat in store.

But who on earth is going to milk her?

The old grey owl answers Who-oo-oo as he flies out through the open half-door of the cowhouse.

# Pay later

WHAT ARE the dead leaves saying?

Old Nart can tell you. They keep falling on the two big dirty-white heaps of sugarbeet, one on each side of the lane leading down to the farm, covering them like a yellow carpet. Their story is an old one, and quite plain to him: *You have been warned.*

It causes him to hobble along a trifle faster, beet-hook in hand, to the ten acres of sugarbeet.

Neither he nor Sam can remember such a season as this, and such weather in October, for getting off the sugar-beet, or for pulling mangolds and sowing wheat and ploughing, and for doing our best—it is never more than that—to keep up with all the never-ending jobs always piling up on the farm.

The work goes well. The wheat is sown. Sam is now ploughing the stubble of Lower Riding for barley. And now, heaven help us, we are faced with the sugar harvest.

This morning there floated through my letterbox a thin yellow slip of paper, itself like an autumn leaf, a receipt from the factory for my first load of this year's beet processed into sugar. It brings me the news that the weight of beet was six tons fourteen hundredweight, the dirt on it ten hundredweight, the clean beet six tons four hundredweight, the sugar 17 per cent, the price 92*s. 6d.*, the load value £28 13*s. 6d.*

It also means that another ton of sugar has gone into the national larder, and let us hope that this will provide a little for Sam and Old Nart as well as for me.

☆

BUT Old (Mark My Words) Nart is not thinking so much about the first load of sugarbeet as the loads still to come. To him the message of the falling leaves is a warning—we must get a move on. Talking to Sam he has a lot to say about what *They* ought to do. By *They* he means the Government or the Minister of Agriculture or the Minister of Food or somebody equally remote from this old Dumpling Field. The things *They* should do are almost as numerous as the autumnal leaves that now litter the lane.

I think perhaps he ought to declare his interest in some of them.

Take pigs, for example. I know he has got some to sell, and he talks about how his old friend Dan Girling sold some old hens and was able to buy twice as many young

18

pigs with the money. Then there is the price of wheat, about half that of malting barley, so no wonder the beer is so dear. And what a job it is to get gumboots, he says, looking down at a well-worn pair.

As for the extra rations now due to the men doing the sugarbeetin' job, where *are* they?

But the sun still shines, the many little pyramids of topped beet are piling up in the field and even Old Nart has to admit there was never such kindly weather for the job.

At least it gives him the opportunity to issue a stern warning to all of us, that this is the kind of weather we shall have to pay for later on.

'You mark my words if we don't,' says Old Nart. As usual, the old man is right. The yellow leaves say so.

# NOVEMBER

*Even in November it is nice to live in a friendly village like ours. Hardly had I left my lane when a voice greeted me over the hedge. 'Come and have a look here,' said Charley Crowe.*

*In his paddock he stood beside a heap of tree trunks and branches, and in one hand held a cross-cut saw, getting ready for log fires. He was so pleased to see me. How could I do other than get hold of one end of the saw for a few minutes as he suggested?*

*An hour or so later it began to rain and I had an excuse to hurry on. Ah . . . there was shelter ahead—Old Ben's barn. From within a welcoming voice boomed, 'Come into the warm and dry; here's a seat for you!'*

*At lunch-time I was still helping Old Ben to pluck his geese. Such a sociable village at this time of year.*

# It's as good as gold!

LITTLE DID we think in our innocence the other day, when Sam and I were spreading muck in the Garbage Field, that a conspiracy was being plotted against us and covetous eyes were watching us through the hedge.

We could understand, of course, any countryman's interest in this job. At this time of year there is no more pleasing sight than a bare stubble dotted over with a symmetrical pattern of black heaps.

For this muck, farmers will tell you, is the mother of money. It is black gold. Where it is spread and ploughed in, if we have any reasonable luck with the weather, we can expect to grow big crops of sugarbeet and potatoes next year.

Just now we are getting ready to plough. The hedges are being trimmed back so that no land is lost and another farming year can begin. An important part of the programme is the muck.

It will put the land, as we say, into 'good heart'. In yet another way it is like gold. It is coveted.

☆

OLD Nart gave us the warning. He happened to overhear a bar-parlour conversation and told us about it.

As we expected, my town friend Herbert was the ringleader. ('He's not daft, by any means,' says Sam.) There he was, having a quiet talk with Sam's next-door neighbour, Joe.

'I walked down the lane this morning,' Herbert begins. He mentions my name. 'He's got plenty of good pig-muck down there,' he goes on. 'They were spreading it on one of the fields.'

Joe sits up and takes notice. 'Well, what d'ye think, is there any chance of a load?'

Herbert winks. 'I know that old so-and-so well. Leave him to me. I'll see what I can do.'

Joe's face brightens. 'That'll be good,' he says. Then he claps his hand on Herbert's knee as he has another inspiration. 'I'll tell you another thing, too. Old Sam's a good old friend of mine. He'll *cart* it for us!'

Herbert rubs his hands. 'There'll be enough for both our gardens,' he laughs.

'Well, same again,' says Joe. 'Here's muck in your eye.'

# This pig could (almost) fly

THE OTHER day, in common with many other farmers in the neighbourhood, I had an urgent SOS from Old Ben asking me to keep a lookout for a big old white boar that had escaped from his farm.

We knew him well by reputation. I can remember Old Ben buying him. It seemed a wise move at the time, because the bacon factory had just announced a special grading scheme, and what weighed most with Ben was that cash deductions were going to be made very shortly for over-fat bacon.

'If you want top price,' a pedigree pig-breeder told him at the time, 'what you want as a boar for your herd is a Landrace.'

☆

So Ben bought *Goteborg Greyhound 31st*. He had a long pedigree and an even longer snout. He was about the size of an elephant, with tusks and memory to match, and he had such a lean and hungry look that (however good he might be for producing lean bacon) all owners of crops and gardens in the vicinity took the view that such boars were dangerous.

Greyhound had a nose for news of any gaps in a hedge. Often, just lately, while we have been drilling the wheat, we have chuckled at the sight of Ben and his man Walter chasing the old pig from one ditch to another.

Then we heard that the boar had put his feet through Ben's garden frames, and a little later Sam saw him running in the meadow with the remains of a clothes-line full of Mrs Ben's washing draped round his neck.

☆

BUT this news of his escape right away from Old Ben's farm was quite a different matter.

It made everybody anxious. For one thing, as Sam pointed out, 'that old boar could move.' (Some said he ought to have gone to Newmarket, and Ben himself agreed that no horse, let alone a man, would have seen him for dust.) It meant that he might be anywhere within miles. He was a real flyer.

But nobody saw him. The net was spread wide; the police were warned and the foot-and-mouth authorities, and search parties organised, but to no avail.

It was not until he was given up for dead that the old boar, gorged and happy, was found fast asleep on a big heap of barley in Old Ben's barn.

# The hedgehog goes a-milking

EVERYBODY AT the Shepherd & Dog blamed Old Nart's pet hedgehog. It would be wrong to say we had a debate. Nobody challenged the verdict that the hedgehog was a sucker.

Long before harvest Old Nart found him as a baby hedgehog in the stackyard, christened him Titus, and taught him to drink milk out of a saucer.

It must be admitted that Titus had his points. He often ate slugs, snails and wireworms. For some time he acted as night-watchman in the garden. Then one day, quite suddenly, he departed.

Not long afterwards Ben's old cow Buttercup just as suddenly lost a quarter. One morning when Ben went to milk her one of her teats was hard and inflamed and gave no milk. When somebody told the veterinary surgeon he said it was mastitis.

We never trust such book learning in farming. 'Mastitis,' roared Ben at the Shepherd & Dog; 'Master Titus, more likely!' He glared at Old Nart: 'Your old hedgehog.'

'They do suck cows,' agreed the blacksmith, 'and after an old hedgehog's once sucked a teat you'll never get any more milk out of it.'

Jim the cowman nodded gravely in support of this traditional explanation for all udder troubles which might otherwise (quite wrongly, of course) be blamed on bad milking.

☆

THEY were all still talking on this prickly subject when Old Nart heard his dog Spot start to bark down the lane. It was just what he had feared. A number of suspicious-looking people had been seen prowling about lately. Somebody was after his turkeys.

He stopped for nothing except to finish his pint and borrow an old shotgun, and then he went shuffling out into the darkness. Sam made a half-hearted offer to go with him, but thought better of it. As he disappeared in the ghostly shadows outside it almost looked as if Old Nart was walking to his doom.

☆

BUT Ben met him in the lane the next day. 'Did you get your thief?' he asked.

For some time Old Nart pretended not to understand, and tried to keep talking about something else, but at last he had to confess. 'It was old Titus come back again,' he said.

It pleased Ben. He looked on it as a kind of revenge for his own misfortune. I think, somehow, he will initiate a debate at the Shepherd & Dog tonight, and that it will be on the question of which is the bigger sucker—the hedgehog or Old Nart.

# Walter's winnings

I MUST give Old Ben his due. It has always been his principle to pay all his small debts promptly and with a good grace.

It has helped his credit and given him a good reputation in the village, and it certainly stood him in good stead in the days when all the old farmers owed a lot of money to the merchants, millers and everybody else. It was a sound idea. 'You see,' he used to explain, 'if you can keep the little dogs from yapping you can keep the big dogs from biting!'

But his all-round man, Walter, had a short, but effective, way of dealing with any undue delay in the paying of his wages. This was simply to walk into the Shepherd & Dog on a Friday night, when it was usually crowded, call for a pint, and say loudly: 'Chalk it up, please: my master hasn't paid me!'

☆

HOWEVER, this week the two of them have been more like brothers than master and man. For it has been a week of suspense for Walter. Since he found out that he was due for a dividend in the treble chance pool he spent sleepless nights wondering what that dividend would be.

But in such anxious times we are friendly people in the countryside. No sooner did the news get round than all his friends (some such old friends that they were almost forgotten) rallied round to cheer him up. 'You'll be worth thousands,' Old Ben told him. And when Ben mentioned something about paying some piece-work money he owed for picking up potatoes, Walter waved a hand and said, 'That'll do some other time.'

☆

IT showed a good spirit. And the next day when Walter was topping sugarbeet so absent-mindedly that he chopped the top off a finger, Ben was first in the field to rush him to the doctor's, and afterwards Ben's missus gave him a cup of 'grandmother's tea' with whisky in it.

They were kindness itself. Even Old Ben's heavy losses in malting barley, calculated by subtracting what he got for it from what he had expected to get, were forgotten for the moment.

As for spending the money, here again help and advice were as abundant as hips and haws on the hedges. Ideas about profitable investments ranged from buying Old Nart's stock turkeys to dealings in millions on the Stock Exchange, and one suggestion was that Walter should buy Old Ben out of his farm.

Meanwhile Walter walked in a dream until he woke one morning to find that his share was five and ninepence!

# The beautiful boar

IN PIG-DEALING the main point is to give satisfaction if you want to keep your customers, though sometimes a little soft soap is helpful.

My friend Mr Podd the pig dealer, more commonly known as Poddy (just as most people in the village are known by some nickname or other), is a pastmaster in the selling art. He can sell anything. He knows how to talk to buyers, and nothing pleases him more than to be able to satisfy them.

But what is giving him particular pleasure at this moment is that he has actually been able to satisfy Old Ben.

The latter, of course, having kept pigs all his life, has an eye for a good pig. And when he recently started keeping a few saddleback sows he let it be known that he was looking for a really good white boar to go with them.

Selecting the right boar, as every pig-breeder will agree, is an important part of the business. He is always said to be 'half the herd'. He is likely to be the father of hundreds or even thousands of bacon pigs.

☆

So the other day, when Poddy took a boar for Ben to have a look at, he met with considerable sales-resistance. 'There you are, sir, a rare long pig,' he said, and reeled off an even longer pedigree. But it was in vain. The boar looked too rough in the coat, and had big 'toshes' or tusks that showed his age. 'I'm not buying a scruffy old thing like that,' declared Old Ben.

The next day Poddy, not to be beaten, had another try to please his difficult customer. I happened to be at Old Ben's farm when he arrived. 'You'll like this one better,' he said.

What a picture of a pig! His snow-white coat shines in the sun. His tail curls beautifully. It is a kind of boar that even Old Ben has to admire, though he tries hard to conceal it. 'That's a bit more like it,' he has to admit, and adds: 'If the price is right.'

'I knew he'd satisfy you,' says the pig dealer, rubbing his hands, and after the usual haggling they clinch the deal.

☆

THEY are both satisfied. Certainly, Poddy is looking pleased enough when he leaves the farm, and he looks even more pleased when I see him later talking and laughing with some of his friends in the Shepherd & Dog.

It had meant trouble—carting the old boar about, removing his 'toshes', rubbing him with soft soap, putting him on plenty of clean wheat straw for a night, and taking him back the next day.

But it was worth it—to satisfy such a customer as Old Ben.

# When a duck
# can skate . . .

THE FIRST time that Sam met the newcomer to the village, Mr Britten the retired schoolmaster, already known to everybody as the Scientific Man, was of course in the Shepherd & Dog.

'He looked', Sam told me, 'just like an old judge with his sparticles on.'

Perhaps it was because all of us on the farms are now engaged in a mad race to get all the land ploughed before Christmas (a golden rule on this heavy clay) that the talk that night in the bar parlour dealt almost exclusively with the weather prospects.

Sam started the argument. 'It's going to be a hard winter,' he announced.

The schoolmaster looked at Sam and nodded. 'I'm convinced you're right,' he said.

Naturally this unqualified support encouraged Sam to say a bit more. 'You've only got to look at all these old red berries on the hedges,' he added.

☆

WE had all noticed this profusion. The idea that it had been specially provided to help the birds through a hard time had never previously been questioned. But Mr Britten dismissed it all as a fairy tale.

'The berries have no significance,' he declared. 'They are the result of the weather we've had. No, the important thing is the temperature of the sea; it's never been really warm this summer, due to the Gulf Stream. It's bound to be a hard, cold winter.'

30

Old Ben's opinion was that all this bad weather was coming from Russia.

But Old Nart, who had been sitting quietly in the corner, was not to be outdone by anybody, least of all a mere stranger to the locality. 'Hold you hard,' he said. 'You ought to have seen my old duck yesterday morning.'

It puzzled our scientific newcomer as to who the 'old duck' might be. But Old Nart goes on: 'Yes, he walked straight over my old pond—it was frozen so hard.'

He pauses to finish his pint. 'That'll prove we shall have a soft winter—you'll see.'

We wait for the inevitable rhyme:

> If the ice in November'll bear a duck,
> The rest of the winter'll be all slush and muck,

recites the old man, triumphantly.

Even the Scientific Man has no reply to that. By popular verdict, Old Nart's duck wins.

# Sausage supper

WHAT A surprise to see my town friend Herbert of all people coming down the snow-covered lane to the farm at this time of the year.

Sam had often invited him. There was the occasion when we badly needed an extra man on the stack for the threshing. There were the freezing days when we were pulling the muddy sugarbeet with a wind-frost raging across the field. Some other more pressing engagement had always kept him away.

Then I saw the boy George smiling and I began to wonder whether there might be some special explanation for this lure of the land in the depth of a hard winter.

It dawned on me. Yesterday the great annual festival, an occasion we had all been looking forward to, had taken place on the farm—the killing of the pig.

31

I saw a big tub and what looked like a stretcher on wooden legs standing outside the pigsty. The butcher came into the yard. His errand was to deal with one of the thirty-three lovely bacon pigs that the boy George had been fattening for our Pig Club with such loving care.

I will spare you the details. Suffice it to say that when I walked into the mealhouse adjacent to the pigsty, which had been temporarily converted into a butcher's shop, I saw the prettiest picture of my farming year.

Even the reddest sunsets, the sunniest scenes of harvest, the coming of the cowslips and primroses along the hedgerows, even the massed beans in full blossom on Clay Hill, could scarcely compare with it.

It was the fat pig, worthy subject for any picture gallery, scraped clean and gleaming white, two hundred odd pounds of pork, bacon, pig's fry and sausages, hanging in two halves from the oak beam above my head.

Sam, too, was admiring it while I enlarged on the prospect of all the brawn and real pork sausages we were planning to make. 'Anybody who does any really hard work on the land,' he said, looking at me thoughtfully and no doubt reflecting that a farm is said to be able to support only one lazy man, 'needs some grub of that sort to put some go into 'im.'

The snow fell and blanketed all the fields in silence and mystery, but the closing rites of the great annual festival were duly observed when Lil and Mary in the farmhouse kitchen took turns in cranking the handle of the sausage machine.

As for the sausage supper which followed, with a full complement of fraternal delegates, including Sam, Old Nart, the boy George and Herbert my town friend, well, once again I will spare you the details in these rationing days.

Let it be enough to say that there is a law of compensation in human affairs which applies even to a life sentence of winter toil on a heavy clay farm. Another sausage? Thank you, I will.

# DECEMBER

*In the big barn I find that Sam, Old Nart, Mary the land-girl and the boy George are sitting very comfortable and warm, walled in with suspended stack-cloths, and with central heat and light provided by a hurricane lantern hanging from a beam. It looks to me like a soft job as well. For they sit side by side and knee-deep in feathers.*

*Everybody's talking turkey. 'Feel the weight of this one,' says Sam. 'Too big for my oven,' says Old Nart. 'Twenty pounds,' guesses the boy George.*

*The feathers fly. Old Nart has his head in clouds of them. Hanging from the rungs of the thatching ladder are rows of plucked turkeys, plump and white in the lamp-light.*

# All hands to the plough

IT IS the unexpected that happens where Old Ben is concerned, and nothing could be more unexpected than the news that he, of all men, had modernised his farmhouse and given his missus every possible labour-saving device to make her life easier.

Naturally it spread quickly through the village, and all the womenfolk praised Old Ben to the skies as a model husband.

It surprised everybody, especially as Ben could hardly be looked upon as a pioneer in farming progress and had been the last in the district to change over to tractors.

We are all on the way to being mechanised now. But the more we mechanise the more we seem to get behind with the work.

☆

TAKE Old Ben. When his father and grandfather farmed this land with horses they had no difficulty in getting it all ploughed before Christmas. In those days they used to say that any farmer worthy of the name ought to polish the breast of his plough and put it away under the bed by Christmas Eve.

Nowadays, with all the tractors, it becomes each year a more desperate race against time.

When I look over the Dumpling Field and see the blue smoke rising where the boy George is now burning the hedge-trimmings, and hear the dull roar of machines from surrounding farms, I know that once again the race is on.

Sam's main anxiety is, of course, to beat Old Ben. There seemed every prospect of success until the other day.

Then it happened. It was a fine frosty morning and there were *three* tractors ploughing in one of Old Ben's fields.

At first he had only one; then somehow he had managed to teach his man Walter to drive. Now there was this mysterious arrival of a third tractor.

In the distance we could just distinguish three stout heavily clothed figures in old Home Guard overcoats squatting on the seats of the tractors and eating up the acres one by one.

'Unfair competition,' snorted Sam. And when he met Ben that night in the village he tackled him about it. 'You're properly goin' in for mechanisation now,' he said.

Old Ben grins. 'Well, I'll tell you the secret,' he replies. 'What's more important than mechanising the farm is to mechanise the farmhouse!'

And he adds: 'Then you can get your missus to come out and sit on the tractor and help to get the ploughing done.'

# Farmyard friends

IT WAS a good day for the farm when the old black cat, Smutty, made it her home.

That was some years ago. I suppose she was intent on solving her housing problems. She did so by curling up and having her four kittens under the wooden manger in my primitive cowhouse, an unpalatial wooden building that had seen better times and housed only Buttercup our house cow.

Occasionally when the sun shone during the summer months and we were trying to gather in the harvest with our old binder, I saw the five of them basking on the straw-strewn cowhouse floor.

The cowhouse was a wise choice for it solved her rationing problems as well. Not only because there was plenty of mice-meat off the ration but also because it was the custom, whether Mary the land girl or Sam was milking, to direct the first stream of Buttercup's milk (which, according to all clean milk rules and regulations, had to be discarded anyway) straight into the old cat's open mouth.

And near the cowhouse door Sam always kept a big tin saucer which he filled with milk for these priority customers to encourage them to stay on the farm.

☆

FORTUNATELY they have made it their home. And now that the dull days get darker and the tumbrils carting off the sugarbeet sink ever deeper into the mud, the five cats plus later additions to their family, have helped us to solve one of *our* problems.

The problem had to do with your sugar ration. Under the dripping elms near the stackyard it was lying out there in the form of white mounds of sugarbeet.

Each morning recently, when Captain and Honey dragged more loads of it through the muddy gateway of the Dumpling Field, we saw that more and more of the beet was being chewed up into shreds of pulp.

Some roots had been hollowed out so that only the thin outer shells remained. Trails of the shredded beet led to round holes in the matted grass in the ditch. Big brown rats had been busy.

I found this out when I walked by night with my dog Sally to take a last look at the farm. We were tramping through the mud in the stackyard when suddenly there was a squeal from high up over the stacks. The sound kept moving about above our heads in the darkness.

I flashed my torch like a searchlight upwards, and a big grey owl flew silently away, dropping a paralysed rat, still squealing, at my feet. When Sally had killed it I saw that its tail was red and raw where the owl had held it. One rat less. There will be fewer still tomorrow and the next day, thanks not only to Sally and the old grey owl, but also to the five cats and their ever-growing family.

There are pin-points of yellow light shining like glow-worms low down in the hedgerows round the Dumpling Field and I know that, watching patiently, keeping guard over the sugarbeet, the five cats and their friends are there.

# Old Ben's treasure island

THE FAITH that moves mountains is in Old Nart. When anything goes wrong, he stands stock-still, lifts a finger, fixes you with his eye, and announces with emphasis: *'There'll . . . be something . . . to put it . . . right.'*

Heaven knows we have need of this assurance often enough. It is a farmer's creed that comforts us in all weathers.

But it hardly seemed necessary yesterday morning. It was just the right weather for ploughing the Dumpling Field. The earth was so frozen that the tractors could chug along comfortably and turn it over in long, square slices that shone like silver in the sunshine.

All the birds of the air seemed to be following the ploughs; flocks of starlings quarrelled over the worms in the fresh furrows; pied wagtails and peewits hunted the clods, and a hundred seagulls hovered over Sam's head as he turned on the headlands.

It looked like a fairy-tale scene and all that we needed, I thought, was the happy ending, when suddenly I saw that Sam had stopped and was bending over his plough. Just our luck—one of the breasts was broken in half.

☆

'Is that the Farmers' Supply Company?' I shouted into the telephone. Yes, they could get me a replacement in a fortnight. The Universal Repairs Incorporated would get it welded for me in a week.

Then Sam suggested: 'What about Old Ben?'

Why hadn't I thought of him? We panted down his lane like diggers in quest of gold.

All round his farmstead—blessed sight—was an assortment of old iron accumulated at farm sales for more years than we can remember.

No Treasure Island could have given Sam such a thrill as this heap of old junk. We were rummaging cheerfully among it when Old Ben appeared, and, on learning our requirements, crawled under a collapsed trailer and came out with just the part we wanted.

Once again a farming miracle had happened to put things right.

# Day of doom

I HAVE always liked a goose for Christmas, but in future I shall settle for a nice piece of pork, thank you. Not that I don't still prefer goose. I like the look of them as fluffy yellow goslings. I admire them when I see them doing the goose step over the green. The one that I select looks even better when it comes steaming out of the oven.

But this year some subversive influence seems to have come over everybody in the village. There are still a few who will pluck turkeys, but nobody who will pluck a goose.

What Old Nart refers to admiringly as the 'real old women' no longer want the job of sitting with a bath in front of them, in a room where you can see nothing but feathers. The young ones say it makes such a mess in the house.

After I had made an unavailing tour of Lesser Snoring with bottles of beer and other gifts as bribes I was forced to the conclusion that I should have to do the job myself, but first I retained Old Nart's services in an advisory capacity.

He watched me begin. 'With geese you have to do *three* pluckings,' he warned.

This startled me. I went on plucking, the wing feathers, and then the breast. After I had done that fairly well I realised that the goose had not only an overcoat but also a waistcoat underneath. And that I should have to go over the carcass again and remove all the down. 'We call it *doom*,' said Old Nart. 'The doom is the devil.' By the time I had finished the second plucking I was in full agreement.

'But what's the third plucking?' I asked.

Old Nart laughed and pointed to my clothes white with down and feathers. 'Pluck yourself!' he said.

# Old Nart lights up

IN THE village only Old Nart can remember as many Christmases as the big old fir tree that stands like a sentinel near the gate of his cottage.

Both of them have seen many changes since the day when Old Nart's beloved mother bought the tree, a very tiny one in a flower pot, from a travelling hawker, and decorated it for Christmas when Nart himself was four.

That expenditure of sixpence was looked upon as extravagance, but Old Nart remembers that it was excused because turkeys had sold so well.

Thereafter the little tree flourished in the garden, in spite of the fact that for several years it was dug up, hung with coloured candles and sugar mice and danced round for a week or so, and then put back again.

☆

BUT for many years now it has grown undisturbed, through wars and peace, seeing the horses give way to tractors, and one generation after another of farmers and farm workers coming and going.

It has become something that we take for granted—a part of the farm, like Old Nart himself—and I have seldom had any occasion to remember it, except when I have walked that way at dusk and startled a pigeon or pheasant out of the tree.

Nor did I know even the history of the tree until the other afternoon, when my last job, before it became dark, was to cut some branches from a holly bush that now shone red in the sunset at the bottom of the Dumpling Field.

☆

It was then that I saw a strange glow, and for a moment I wondered if Old Nart's cottage was on fire. With my sack of holly I walked that way. Yes, something was happening there. As I turned the corner of the lane I saw the tree— Nart's old tree—a mass of red and green and yellow lights, blazing like a beacon in the gloom.

Looking up at it stood an old grey-bearded figure—Old Nart himself. The lights gleamed on his weathered face and I could see him smiling at his own thoughts.

It was a rehearsal of the celebrations that the old man was planning for Christmas. And I could almost swear that there were tears in his eyes.

# He's a kind old hoss

Old Captain stands motionless in the strawed yard adjoining the stable, with his head lowered almost to his knees, a living symbol of that greatest farming virtue, patience.

He has had his Christmas dinner of chaff and corn, and Sam has stuffed his rack like a Christmas stocking with clover hay.

Sometimes I have found him standing like this, in the middle of the night, when Sam and I with my dog Sally have been out late looking for rats. I have often wondered what the old horse is thinking about when he stands there in the yard so silent and so still. Does his memory go back all of twenty-three years to the summer when he frisked about as a foal with his mother on the meadow?

Since then he has learned every job on the farm and now that he is getting old, and stumbles and nods as he walks in front of the harrows, patience is written on every wrinkle of his shiny brown coat.

Patiently he has stood in the shafts of the big waggon through the sometimes sweltering heat of harvest, moving from shock to shock of the sheaves at the call of the hold-ye boy.

Patiently he has pulled the muddy tumbril from heap to heap of the topped sugarbeet through the wind-frost and biting winds of drab December days.

'HE'S a kind old hoss,' says Sam, and no greater compliment could be paid. We owe him a lot, not only for the acres he has ploughed and drilled and horse-hoed, and the harvests he has helped to get in, but also for the example he sets to everybody.

For if ever Sam or I get anxious about the coming of the threshing machine, or about when the lorry will be taking away some more sugarbeet, or how on earth we are going to find feed for the pigs, all we have to do is to go and have a word with Captain.

He turns his old head round as if to say: 'Don't worry, it isn't worth it.'

But there are two things that Captain does not like. One is dragging the noisy water-cart when the water splashes his legs, and the other is pigs.

No war-time rationing or restrictions upset him. Nobody has ever seen him kick. Nothing, not even doodle-bugs buzzing over the farm during the war or low-flying fighters over the fields, ever made him turn a hair.

41

But when we quartered some of Susan the Sow's piglets in temporary pens in the horseyard Captain was quite annoyed. He chased the young pigs whenever they ventured through the palings. He snorted at the sows.

After the pig-dealer had arrived and we had higgled and haggled, nobody was more pleased than Captain when a lorry came the next day and took away a load of little pigs, and left him in peace again.

For pigs come and go, and wars too, for that matter, but Sam's old horse Captain, stumbling over the clods, seems to go on for ever.

# Parsnip wine

AFTER DARK on Boxing Day it has long been Sam's custom to take a walk over the fields to Old Ben's farm.

Once again this year I could follow his progress in that direction by the flickering light of the old hurricane lantern that he always carried on these convivial occasions. I could imagine the two of them there, crouched over the log fire, rivalry forgotten, smoking their pipes and sipping Old Ben's famous parsnip wine.

Sam could leave without more than the usual anxiety inseparable from a farm. The pigs and the old mare, Honey, had been fed; the sows were snoring in the straw, and Judy had been milked. The only doubtful factor was Susie the young gilt, soon expecting her first litter of pigs. Even that problem has been entrusted to safe hands in Old Nart. That Worthy had already given his verdict. 'P'raps she will and p'raps she won't,' he had said and promised to have another look before midnight.

So there was nothing much to worry about. They discussed the weather, the fact that all their fields were ploughed in good time, the way the drains were running, and the prospects for next harvest. The more wine Sam drank the better he felt those prospects would be.

THIS year Ben produced for Sam's inspection his Christmas present, a big green parrot in a wire cage that his nephew had brought him from overseas.

They kept talking till nearly midnight, at which hour (according to Old Ben) all kinds of strange ghosts walked the farm, including an old white sow with a clanking chain which Sam would probably meet on his way home. It reminded Sam about Susie. So, after having 'one for the mud,' he took leave of a friendly host and set off back over the fields.

There was a dim light in the piggeries. A bearded figure stood there, leaning over Susie's sty. 'How is she?' gasped Sam.

'She's pigged,' said the old man. And, while Sam was vainly trying to count them, he added: 'Nine good pigs, a New Year present for you.'

Then Old Nart stared at Sam for a moment and laughed so loud that Susie jumped up with a snort and an old owl glided away from a beam overhead. 'And not the only one you've got, I see,' he said, pointing.

In Sam's hand, instead of the hurricane lantern, was a green parrot in a cage.

# JANUARY

No sooner had the last load of sugarbeet left the lane than my town friend Herbert came to pay one of his rare January visits to the farm.

Sam welcomes him. 'Come and have a look at my bullocks,' he says.

No wonder Sam is proud of them. Their red coats shine as though painted in oils; they get fatter every day. As for the rustling straw beneath them it is not only a reminder of last harvest but a rich promise for the next, in loads of precious muck to come out of this yard.

Naturally all this prime beef impresses Herbert. Even if he cannot take any away with him, his visit is not entirely in vain, for he leaves with nearly enough good muck on his boots to start his own farm.

# Where's the bull?

THE AUCTIONEER, standing high up in the old farm waggon, smiles at the crowd of farmers gathered round. 'Now let's have the bull,' he says. Two men make for the farm buildings to obey his command.

All the cows have been sold. I thought the auctioneer had exhausted all his superlatives in describing them. But he has some left for the bull and while we wait he gives the pedigree and history of this remarkable animal in full. 'Plenty of milk, gentlemen,' he observes.

My town friend Herbert is a little surprised at this remark. I have to explain that, like the well-known advertisement of 'bull for sale, dam good milker,' it really means the good milk performance is that of his dam.

☆

THERE'S Charley Crowe over there with Old Ben. Everybody seems to be at this sale. The Major is talking to Tommy Dodd. And there's Sam. It's probably because the work is so well forward on all the farms.

The weather, of course. While we are waiting we learn of somebody who has seen a cowslip in bloom, of a farmer who has some self-sown barley actually in ear, and another with a field of beans already half-way to harvest.

The auctioneer is getting a little impatient now. 'Bring out the bull,' he shouts.

Old Nart is here with me. I had thought it only right that he should have a change. While I was away he spent Christmas alone on my one-horse farm. It was a period of perfect peace for him. On my return yesterday my first question was: 'Well, did you have a good time?'

'Yes, that I did,' he said with emphasis. 'I sat over there

all the time,' indicating his cottage with a wave of his arm, 'and never saw a soul.'

He is making New Year resolutions now and I think I know what one of them is likely to be.

For while we keep talking the auctioneer is getting more and more exasperated. 'Where's that bull?' he roars.

☆

'COMING, sir!' says a voice. There is yelling from the direction of the buildings. Yes, the bull *is* coming. His bull staff, fixed to a ring in his nose, drags in the mud. Weighing nearly a ton, he is coming straight for us at full gallop.

One moment there is a great crowd. The next there is nobody in sight. It happens as suddenly as that. From my post behind a hedge I see Old Nart peeping round the barn door. Everybody else has gone.

The only exception is the auctioneer, left alone on the waggon and waving his hammer. 'Someone get hold of him,' he shouts.

As for Old Nart, it has given him such a shock that his first resolution for 1954 is to stay at home in splendid isolation and keep away from bull sales.


# Bella's fur coat

THE CHANCES of Charley Crowe's wife, Bella, getting her fur coat seem to have improved considerably with the coming of the New Year.

It is a subject that has taken up much of our attention in recent debates at the Shepherd & Dog. Doubtless her idea at one time was a rabbit-skin coat. But now myxomatosis disease has ended that dream for the time being, and even rabbit pie isn't being talked about.

Yet when one gate of opportunity shuts on a farm, another usually opens to us.

ONCE again—luckily for Bella—that is exactly what has happened. The first stories of the new arrivals came from my old friend Adam, the roadsweeper. He had seen huge brown rats dragging whole sugar beet off the fields. Then the postman reported having seen a strange animal—at first mistaken for an otter—swimming in the stream at the bottom of the Dumpling Field. Old Ben was the next witness. Half his sugar beet crop had been devoured, according to him. Evidently the newcomer had a sweet tooth.

Arguments about the size of the animals would have done credit to an anglers' annual dinner. Some said they were bigger than hares. Mr Podd, the pig dealer, had shot one, three feet long. As for the one that got away, well. . . .

Our schoolmaster, of course, at once identified the specimen. '*Coypu* or *nutria*,' he said, 'a South American rodent.'

Then came the news that Bella's husband Charley had got five of them at one go with his 12-bore. 'They tell me they *eat well*,' laughs Charley. But Bella is thinking of something much more important than that.

# The slim pig

THE BIG marquee is packed with farmers. They are at school again. The lesson (you will be pleased to hear) is on how to produce Leaner Bacon. Yes, a bacon pig demonstration. There are a lot of them taking place up and down the country today.

There are live bacon pigs here as well. You can see them in the audience quite clearly, in strawed pens. They are all here, pigs and farmers, to try to please the housewife. There is such a crowd that chairs have been put up the aisle as at a harvest thanksgiving. Farmers are sitting all round the pigs. They are anxious to learn, and none more so than Old Ben.

The idea of feeding the people properly appeals to him greatly, as also does the special bonus for Grade 'A' bacon. He sits there with Old Nart, facing the platform, on which there are some very important people, including a manager of a bacon factory.

A LECTURER from the National Agricultural Advisory Service is speaking. He is pointing out how we can recognise the signs of leaner bacon in the *live pigs*. To make it even clearer, above each pen of pigs hangs (alas, my poor brother!) a half-carcass of a pig freshly killed from the same litter.

'Much too fat,' he is saying, looking at the factory manager but referring to one of the pens of porkers. 'Look at the thick, coarse shoulders. Those pigs will grade badly. And the bacon, as you see, is just what housewives don't want nowadays. Look at the belly fat.'

Then he turns to another group of pigs. 'That's the bacon type,' he observes. 'Note the fine shoulder and the length. They'll grade well. Look at the carcass.

'Breeding counts, of course,' he goes on. 'And a lot depends on feeding. A good plan is never to give pigs more than 6lb of food a day.' At this, one of the baconers starts squealing and others grunt in protest. But soon, as the lecturer drones on, they are all snoozing again in the straw.

The lecture seems to be having a similar effect on Old Ben. He begins to snore, and then surprises all of us by suddenly waking up with a loud yell.

He explained to Old Nart afterwards that he had dreamt that the pigs had got control of the meeting and were making practical bacon demonstrations on the farmers and particularly on him.

Old Nart listened with amusement, but he had only one comment. 'I shouldn't imagine you graded very well,' he said.

# Night call

TROUBLES NEVER seem to come singly on Old Ben's farm. When I went to see him about a week ago he seemed most cheerful. I sat down opposite him by the old log fire in the kitchen while his missus opened a bottle of her parsnip wine.

I thought what a model husband he was, sitting there in his slippers. It was common knowledge in the village that he had turned over a new leaf. His missus is really the boss (he owes a lot of his success in life to that fact) and this New Year she made one very good resolution for him.

It was that he should give up going to the Shepherd & Dog and stay at home and be satisfied with her home-made wine.

For the first week he hardly left his lane. Even when his last load of sugarbeet went to the factory—a farming event above all others that calls for some celebration—he failed to appear in the bar parlour. I had begun to wonder if he was ill. My visit reassured me. But I had not been there very long before this scene of domestic peace was shattered by a knocking at the door.

☆

WHEN Old Ben hurried to open it he looked extremely surprised to see his right-hand man Walter, standing there.

'What's the matter?' asked Old Ben.

Walter told him: 'Your old cow Snowdrop's been taken queer. Looks as if she's got wooden tongue or even foot-and-mouth,' he added with a groan.

'Dear, dear,' muttered Old Ben, turning to his missus. 'Well, I suppose I'd better go and see the vet about her.'

I knew the cow. Bought after he had sold Buttercup, the old white cow was one of the best Ben has ever had. I could understand his anxiety, as he put on gumboots and followed Walter out into the dark and wintry night.

☆

STRANGELY enough, Sam witnessed the same thing when he went to see Old Ben last night.

The same unexpected knock on the door, almost the same message from Walter (except that it was milk fever this time) and the same hurry to go and see the vet. It was bad luck. Naturally, when I met Mrs Ben this morning I took the first opportunity to ask after the old cow and to sympathise.

'Poor old Snowdrop, indeed!' she said grimly. 'She had to wait a rare long time while Ben was going for that vet, I can tell you.'

There was a hard glint in her eyes.

51

# Sam's shruff shed

SAM, LIKE most sons of the soil, is a man of few words. But they are words that mean something. I have known him solve many a farming problem with a word of one syllable.

'What we shall have to do,' he said the other day when we were faced with one of these problems, 'is to build an old Shruff Shed.'

It was a new word to me, but somehow it seemed, like many others in a countryman's vocabulary, to explain itself. In my mind I could see the shed; it was already built, and sheltering the old sows from the sun.

We had been discussing turning out our herd of pigs in summer on Clay Hill. There will be plenty of good grazing there on the lucerne, grasses and clover that flourish on this fourteen acres. There is a stream and a pond.

Having all these sows there will add fertility to the field, to say nothing of cash to my banking account. But there is no shelter. We could put up an elaborate building or make one of baled straw; either way would be expensive now that we are short of straw. Why, of course, the obvious answer is Sam's idea—*the Shruff Shed*.

☆

So today Sam, Old Nart and the boy George are doing two jobs at once. They are chopping down a high hedge that darkens the Dumpling Field. As Sam says—'That'll let the daylight in.'

In these grey days we welcome any hint of future sunshine once again flooding the fields. These winter jobs of cutting down hedges and clearing out ditches fortunately have a link with the brighter days ahead. They are a preparation for the time (not far distant) when we shall see the primroses, the dust rising behind the drill and the seed going in.

But in cutting down this hedge we have another purpose. It is to tie these trimmings and branches into bundles or 'faggots', such as once were used for the old brick ovens where our grandmothers baked bread.

There is already a pile of them on the headlands where the wheat lies under a blanket of snow. When they are carted down to Clay Hill, and bound tightly together round a framework of stouter wood, they will make a good shelter for the old sows while they graze there in the summer months.

Yes, sometimes these dull days are dreary enough. But helping to bind up the faggots brings with it a picture of my black-and-white pigs quietly grazing against the background of green lucerne and blue sky, while I sit idly smoking a pipe in Sam's old Shruff Shed.


# Pot luck

THE STOCK pot hangs from an iron hook in the big open chimney. Into it Walter, or Old Soldier, as we sometimes call him, pops various odds and ends of vegetables, meat scraps and bones from time to time. A rabbit, a pigeon or two, plenty of onions and carrots find their way into it on occasions. Sometimes it simmers away merrily with a log fire under it, and sometimes it cools and is forgotten for days.

For Old Soldier (a survivor from some old war) lives by himself in a cottage on the green that has few modern advantages. The only water and light come through the roof. But he has some compensations.

Now in the middle of winter jasmine and snowdrops

brighten his garden; and occasionally, if you walk that way and the wind is in the right quarter, a delicious smell comes to you.

☆

HERBERT, my town friend, has good cause to sniff at it. His wife is away and for a few days he has had to look after himself. A diet of hard-boiled eggs is beginning to pall. Yet he puts a good face on it as he sits in the tap room at the Shepherd & Dog. 'I can't see why there should be all this fuss about cookery,' he argues. 'I find it simple enough.'

A voice from the corner interrupts him. 'If you want really good meals, there's only one thing for it, and that's a stock pot.' It is Walter, the old soldier.

He and Herbert are at once on common ground. They compare experiences. At the end of it Walter makes a most friendly offer. 'Come and have a snack with me,' he says. 'You'll have to take pot luck, of course.'

The pot is simmering when they reach the kitchen. The table is soon spread for the guest. With a triumphant flourish his host dips a big ladle into the stew. 'Now you'll see,' he boasts. 'Hold out your plate.' He fills it with one great scoopful.

For a tense moment there is silence. Then there is a muffled exclamation from Herbert. The old soldier looks at his guest and then at the plate.

'I wonder how long that's been there?' he says.

They are both staring at the mouse in the stew.

# FEBRUARY

*In the field called Lower Riding, which adjoins Old Ben's farm, we made a mistake last year. We stole a march on him and sowed our barley long before he had even prepared a seed-bed. For miles round it was the only field sown. From miles round the crows settled on it in swarms. We must not do that again.*

*We must wait for Old Ben. Sam and I watch him, on his field opposite, trying to make up his mind, kicking a clod or two, dragging a foot through the soil. In fact he makes every test except the real one recommended by our fore-fathers—taking off one's trousers and sitting down bare on the good earth. If it strikes cold, don't sow, they said.*

*Whatever happens, we are not sowing until he does. For we are all for fair shares—of crows and of corn.*

# Man of the hour

WHEN THE hooter of Old Ben's car went wrong the obvious thing was to go and see Tommy Dodd.

Every village has its handyman, but it is a fortunate village that has one like him. He is a man of many parts. Most of them lie on the table in the cottage living-room which serves as his workshop.

There you may see ten or more clocks or watches or wireless sets in every stage, either of being taken to pieces or (less frequently) of being put together again.

One of his business maxims is never to throw anything away ('it may come in handy for something'), so that if you want, say, a new bulb for a torch he may have to try a score or so before he finds one that has not been used and discarded by previous customers. Yet he always gets results. Some, it is true, are not quite what we expect. This is probably due to some error on the part of the manufacturer of the article under repair. As Tommy often points out: 'It wasn't made right in the first place.'

THAT was his explanation after Sam's wireless had been mended, with the result that it now has to be turned on whenever he wants to turn it off.

But these are minor matters. The main consideration in our village is that Tommy exists; if he didn't we should have to invent him. For now that this new era of mechanisation has come to the farms, it is vital that we should have somebody on the spot prepared to take anything to pieces at all times, whether it is necessary or not.

That hour has come—and with it the man.

What is even better, his example is spreading. I saw the boy George this morning hanging by one arm like a monkey

from a beam in the cowhouse roof, tracing a 'short' in the electric wiring. What a miracle, I thought, that everybody, apart from Old Nart, has adapted himself so readily to mechanisation.

No sooner had this struck me than something also struck the boy George, for, in a flash of blue flame, he fell with a yell into the manger. But whatever shook him did not shake my conviction.

Then there is Sam, brought up with horses, who now handles electric levers with the indifference of Ajax playing about with lightning, and sometimes with equally spectacular results.

Old Ben, too, is converted to the new ways. I can see that plainly in his happy smile as he comes back down the lane in his car, pleased that the mended hooter now keeps hooting *all the time*, so that now he has music wherever he goes.

# One of the few

COMING INTO the warmth of the shepherd's hut wrought a transformation in Old Nart.

Once again he was a shepherd's boy (or 'page', to use the correct term) and imagined that the shepherd sitting opposite him by the stove suddenly had a smock and a black beard and was his friend Amos of sixty years ago.

It all came back to Old Nart. There was Amos, fumbling with a piece of paper. It was a leap year and one of the dairymaids who was friendly with Amos had sent him a most important letter—asking him to marry her.

As Amos could neither read nor write, the boy Nart had to read it to him—after the shepherd had made him put wool in his ears to prevent him hearing what he was reading.

And Amos had insisted on answering it himself. Carefully he scrawled a big 'I' such as he used to record the birth of each lamb, and then pasted next to it a lump of wool from the back of one of his old ewes.

☆

WHAT a shepherd he was. At lambing time the only sleep he had for weeks would be an occasional doze in his bunk or beside the fire. He was always alert in any emergency. Sometimes the ewes had twins or triplets, even quads or quins. And Amos, who usually had about 300 ewes under his care, never had fewer than 450 lambs from them.

At about a month old the lambs' tails were removed to prevent them from getting bedraggled in the mud. It was 'tailing time', the shepherd's harvest, when Amos had his bonus of sixpence a tail.

Sheep are on the increase again, but nowadays there are few shepherd families such as those that once handed down their skill from father to son.

☆

No wonder the lambing yard, with its cosy pens built of straw bales (quite an unusual sight these days), had made such an appeal to Old Nart and that the shepherd's welcome: 'Come and sit by the stove'—had been so readily accepted. As of old, there was the low bunk, the sick lamb by the fireside, the chair and table, the milk warming on the stove. It was snug there and made the old man doze and dream.

When the shepherd's wife came in bringing tea (with a little something in it to keep out the cold) and asked him to have some, his thoughts were still with Amos and the completely satisfactory answer he had given to the love-letter.

'I wool,' smiled Old Nart.

# Sam saves his bacon

I FOUND my first primrose the other day in a sheltered spot near the old moat.

It lured me into a grave error. It was a spring-like day and in the sunshine a pair of moorhens clucked around, looking for a place to build their nest. The snow had gone and the snowdrops had come. So I made the fatal mistake of talking to Sam about sowing the spring corn.

'Life is sweet, brother,' I said to myself. 'Day and night, brother, both sweet things.' I had overlooked the wind on the heath.

That came later. It grew with such violence and roared through the elms until, when night fell, all the farm moaned and groaned in the grip of the gale.

As always on a farm, troubles did not come singly. That very night my young sow Susan decided to have her first litter of pigs.

Now pigwifery under any circumstances is a fine art. With the storm threatening to take the roof off, it became a nightmare. But little pigs are like nuggets of gold these days, and Sam and I took it in turns to keep an avaricious eye on Susan.

We depended on her. We knew what a difference it would make (when the young pigs came to be sold as weaners in eight weeks time) if she had two or ten on this momentous occasion.

☆

As Sam says as an excuse for pigs: 'After all, they're only human.' No sooner are they born than they are ready to push through a crowd to find a long drink and a warm corner at the bar.

We had ample warning of this event. During the afternoon Susan spent most of her time walking about with mouthfuls of straw and making a bed. Now, through a convenient spyhole in the sty wall, we watched the little pigs being born one by one, sometimes at short intervals and sometimes with an hour between births.

Precious pigs. The gale roared, Susan alternately snorted and snored, and our spirits soared as the litter number went up. There were eight, there were ten. At the eleventh hour came the eleventh pig.

It seemed to be as much as Susan could stand. She got up and threw her customers in all directions. I knew then what a litter meant. They were littered all over the sty.

When she lay down again there were ten. One was buried under a quarter-ton of bacon. It was nearly as flat as a pancake when Sam rescued it. And not even the wind outside blew so persistently as Sam did into the lungs of this piglet as he applied artificial respiration. It came to life. At dawn, although the top of the barley stack was in the horsepond, we smiled because the golden little pigs had been saved.

# Pounds, shillings and pigs

NOWADAYS EVEN small farmers like Old Ben (and I use 'small' in the acreage sense only) have to be higher mathematicians as well as ploughmen and cowmen.

I seldom see him during these grey depressing February days, but occasionally I do glance over the dull fields at the ancient monument that is his farm, mainly because it comforts me to think he is probably working there in even stickier mud and a bigger muddle than we are.

Like me, he lives at the end of a muddy lane that at this season of the year effectively isolates him from everybody except tax collectors, and recent weather has made this isolation even more complete.

So naturally Sam and I were surprised the other morning when we saw quite a stream of expensive-looking traffic making tracks for Old Ben's farm.

It puzzled us so much that, having nothing more useful to do, I took a walk in that direction. But when I arrived all the cars had gone, and I found Old Ben sitting in his kitchen biting a pencil and absorbed in complex calculations.

Was it pay-as-you-earn? Or was Ben trying to work out the new system promised by the Government of complete freedom for farmers with guaranteed prices and assured markets thrown in?

Then he enlightened me. 'I've sold nearly all them pigs,' he said.

☆

I REALISED how much the pig trade was looking up when we went out a few minutes later and found that another Rolls-Royce had arrived.

Its occupant, as portly as Old Ben himself, walked into the last yard of pigs remaining for sale. He and Ben counted them carefully. Yes, twenty-seven.

'A good class of pig,' said the dealer. 'Very nice.' It seemed almost reluctantly that he mentioned that three were 'a trifle small'. I could see the pig trade was booming.

Then he went straight to the point. 'I'll give you seven pounds five shillings each for the twenty-four and six pounds each for the small ones,' he said.

It seemed a good price to me, and I believe Old Ben thought so, too. But he shook his head and stood waiting for another offer.

It came. 'Very well, I'll make it seven pounds seven and six for the big'uns and five each for the three small'uns. How's that?'

It sounded better and Ben accepted it. I left him deep in his pigonometry again.


# The pole's here

A TALL, dark stranger stands in the lane leading to the farm, taking notes.

More trouble, I say to myself. What is it this time—the rates or the income tax?

That's the mood Old Nart and all of us are in at the moment. Everything has gone wrong. My few hens have stopped laying and my solitary sow Susan has been so disgruntled just lately that she has even stopped to sniff twice at her swill.

The outlook has been grim, and Old Nart has been trying to make it worse. Only this morning he pointed out to me a patch of dirty snow still remaining, like a split bag of fertiliser, in the ditch, 'You know what that's doing?' he asked.

I pretend I don't, just to humour him, and he trots out the familiar answer. 'That's waitin' for some more!'

62

As if we hadn't had enough already. But one of the great blessings of farming is that when everything looks blackest something invariably happens to cheer us up.

☆

AND it does once again. Ah, yes, you will say—the primroses. Or the snowdrops and aconites now making a yellow-and-white carpet round the old moat. The longer, lighter days; the promise of the coming of spring.

They all help. But even they are forgotten in an event that now surprises the village. The stranger has a short stake in his hand. 'I'm wondering where I should put the pole,' he says.

I glance down what is really the village high street. Something exciting seems to be happening. Little groups of womenfolk are out at their gates.

It comes to me in a flash. 'Put the pole anywhere you like,' I hasten to reply; 'and now you're here, come in and have some fatted calf.'

We have been waiting for him for a long time. In the village everybody is smiling as if spring had already come. Even Susan (think of it, infra-red lamps for her little pigs!) grunts a welcome to this unexpected visitor from the Electricity Board.

# Beer—or sausages?

COME AND sit on this old oak settle beside the log fire at the Shepherd & Dog and listen to Old Nart. I know no better remedy for wintry weather.

He is talking about sowing the spring barley. It conjures up a delightful vision. As he talks the snow melts away and the winter passes. I see the sun shining on the golden seed as it pours down into the soil. And the dust rises behind the drill.

What a picture! Even the old man is inspired by it. The

dust rises so much that it gets into his throat and he keeps coughing until I stand him another pint.

It refreshes him for another dissertation on the merits of early sowing. 'As soon as it's dry enough so we can get on to the land we must make a start,' he declares. Then he turns to Sam. 'What sort of barley are you going to grow this year?' he asks.

'Barley for sausages,' Sam tells him; 'for feeding pigs.'

The new sausages, made from real pork. It conjures up an even more delightful vision. We can smell them as they sizzle.

'All the old farmers ought to grow feeding barley,' says Jim the cowman, 'if we're going to keep on feeding all these pigs.'

'If they do, what shall we use for beer?' demands Old Ben.

WE must choose, it seems, between beer and sausages. But talking of beer launches Old Nart on another story of the old-time brewer who used to drive round all these inns in a pony-cart to sell his famous 'tuppenny ale'.

'Any people been drunk?' he asked on one occasion. No, they told him, but two customers had burst.

But Sam thinks there never was such a thing as bad beer; his only problem, as with the new sausages, is the price.

Old Ben, whose cow, Buttercup, is now doing five gallons a day, expresses the opinion that milk ought to be the same price as beer.

'Better still,' chuckles Old Nart, 'if sausages and beer were the same price. Twopence a skinful.'

Perhaps that was what he had eventually, as the beer and sausages argument went on. For it seems that late that night (if Sam is to be believed) Old Nart took a short cut in the dark across the meadow where the cows had been. He lost his cap and, so Sam tells me, had to try on five or six before he found the right one!

# MARCH

*There are primroses in the ditches along the lane, but it still rains, and we are having breakfast in the barn. Old Nart, as usual, is talking about the weather.*

*'You watch those old seagulls,' he says. 'When they fly north you can depend on fine weather. When they go south it means storms.'*

*'Then there's the old rooks. When you see them goin' round in circles high up—winding up the clock, as the saying is—you always get rain.'*

*'There's another thing about them,' he goes on. 'Have you seen them carrying sticks to their nests this year?' Sam has to admit he has not.*

*'Nor have I,' says Old Nart, 'and what's more, we shan't get any good weather until they do.'*

*Sam takes another look out at the rain, hoping to see an old rook carrying a stick away with him, high up into the trees.*

# Ben borrows a hen

OLD BEN has always been one to take care of the pence. Probably this explains his success on quite a small farm.

Ben's old hen, as everybody now refers to it, will go down in village history as a good example of the way he has done it.

One day last month he left his lane to go to see a lady on the green who kept geese. After a lot of haggling he bought six goslings at ten bob apiece. He did not like paying the price but there was no option. Everybody wanted goslings. They would keep the grass down and do the office of a scythe under the orchard trees. They would grow fast and get fat without any expensive feeding. People, he thought, would want fats next winter. The geese would make a good price (on some market, black or otherwise) at Christmastime. The lady who sold them certainly encouraged that hope. According to her, only the sky would be the limit.

An old speckled hen was strutting about with the goslings. She had hatched them out and now marched them about like a sergeant with an awkward squad. It was agreed, on Old Ben's suggestion, that he could borrow the hen for a time just to keep the goslings together.

So the goslings went and lived on Ben's grass and grew so fast that they were soon as big as their foster-mother.

☆

THIS happened at about the time he said he was retiring from farming. He thought he ought to take things a bit easier, and he was not getting any younger.

A lot of his old cronies, Sam among them, went to see him after he had made that decision. They wanted to see how he was spending his spare time. He was spending it as they expected. They walked into his yard to find him feeding pigs; he had bought another couple of sows. When they looked over his hedge they saw him chopping out sugarbeet. He had taken on a new contract for growing some more peas. He still kept his cows and retailed the milk, and was rearing a few heifers as well. They realised he would as soon give up breathing as give up farming.

Then they saw the old hen with the goslings. Ben was still keeping it. It was Sam who reminded him that it was about time to send it back to the lady who owned it.

'Hold you hard,' said Ben; 'we don't want to be in any hurry to do that.' He nudged Sam and winked.

'The old hen has started to lay,' said Ben.

# Pig palace

I WASN'T surprised to see Old Nart hobbling down the lane on his way to hospital the other morning.

His rheumatics have been shocking lately. His cottage is a condemned one; it has water laid on through the roof. Townspeople who come in the summer call it picturesque. They don't know that it has no damp course.

I cannot help contrasting it with the pig palace now occupied by my sow, *Landrace Lucy 1st*, more usually known as *'Go-through-a-Mortal-lot'*, which better describes her capabilities. There she lies in luxury. No absence of a damp course is allowed to inconvenience her. Even the floors have been specially insulated against damp and cold. A low false roof of straw keeps the warmth in. She has all mains services, and in the corner, her recently born litter of twelve is cosily sleeping under the rays of an infra-red lamp.

THIS is not, perhaps, so surprising. They used to say in the village that if a child were ill somebody came along in an Austin Seven. If it were a pig, a whole lot of officials came—in Rolls-Royces.

I saw Old Nart on his way back from the hospital, and asked him how he'd got on. He looked better already.

'I shall be all right now,' he said, grinning. 'It's proper up-to-date treatment they give you up there. Pity that Health Scheme didn't come in fifty year ago.

'What do you think?' he went on. 'You'd hardly believe it. Put me under one o' them there infra-red lamps, they did, same as you've got for that old sow.'

# 'Scruffy'

WHENEVER I saw my old dog Scruffy tottering about, nearly blind and quite deaf, I thought of the days when she was in her prime and used to hunt rabbits alongside the deep ditch at the bottom of the Dumpling Field.

She enjoyed it, but she was never a success as a hunter,

and I think the rabbits enjoyed it quite as much as she did. But it was her happy hunting ground. It was a common sight then to see her excitedly bouncing up and down like an india-rubber toy beside that hedge. We can comfort ourselves now that she has had her good times on the farm.

For yesterday old Scruffy (she was seventeen years old) disappeared.

While we hunted for her we kept remembering more and more of the old dog's history as hopes of finding her grew less and the sun sank, our hearts with it.

Sam could remember vividly the Christmas Day when he had to rush out from his dinner to chase an old sow that had invaded his garden (the kind of thing that happens on feast days and other solemn occasions) and returned to find his pudding—with the rum on it!—gone, and Scruffy licking her lips.

ALL such exploits are now forgiven. Today we have only one thought. Everybody on the farm joined in a last hunt for the old lady.

Round the barns and buildings; surely, decrepit as she was, she couldn't have gone far. But of late she had seemed a bit light-headed. 'Perhaps she went sannakin' off somewhere,' guessed Sam.

It was the boy George who first heard the feeble bark. We slipped and stumbled over the muddy furrows in that direction. Then we all heard it, more plainly. It was over the field, by the hedge.

At the bottom of that ditch, at the very spot where she and her daughter Sally had spent so many happy hours hunting, we found old Scruffy. Sam lifted her out of the mud and water.

She now lies sleeping, warm and dry, in her basket in the farmhouse kitchen and, judging by her twitching tail and the happy look on her face, I imagine she is dreaming of hunts by the hedge in the Dumpling Field.

# A black look for Old Ben

IF OLD BEN'S farm had been located in Darkest Africa he could hardly have had a more frightening experience than he had the other evening.

Tired after a long day of walking behind the drill, sowing barley, he was sitting by his log fire reading about Mau Mau when it happened.

That particular day, even on my small farm, had been an eventful one. It was the first day of the spring sowings. Old Nart was my master of ceremonies. He had ordained that his own job should be to borrow a drill, a pair of horses and the boy George and get my spring wheat in. He had reserved for me the privilege of sowing the slag in front of the drill.

For this job a man walks the furrows like an old-time sower. A heavy, loaded pail is suspended from a strap round his shoulders, leaving his hands free to fling the magic powder in a semi-circular shower in front of him, and his thoughts free to curse the inventor of such a primitive system, as he staggers along.

What he looks like at the end of a day depends on the fertiliser. And slag makes him look like a sweep.

☆

THIS slag-sowing job is to be mine. Over a ton of it is set out in sacks across the field.

I hear a voice at my shoulder. 'Want any help?' it asks. It is Old Ben's missus, who is as strong as any horse. I offer her the job. 'Equal pay for equal work on *this* farm,' I assure her.

Mrs Ben jumps at the chance. Nothing seems to worry her—not even the slag.

It is nearly dark when we finish the field and Ben's missus goes home.

They are all laughing and talking scandal when I reach the Shepherd & Dog a little later. 'Old Ben's got a black woman now,' declares Tommy Dodd. 'I saw her go into his house tonight when I passed.'

I heard afterwards from Old Ben himself what a shock he got when his missus walked in.


# Second thoughts

WE HAD a long debate in the stable the other morning, with Captain and Honey and Old Don listening in, about what on earth we could grow on the odd quarter-acre that had been left unsown in the corner of the ploughed-up meadow.

With this trifling exception all our fields and crops had been sown. It had been, as usual, a mad scramble. We had sown what we could, where we could, when we could, and as fast as we could. One day saw the barley go in on Big Smithies; on the next we drilled the sugarbeet on High Riding; on yet another we planted the potatoes. So it went on, and in the dusk of each evening, while we unharnessed the old horses and puffed at our pipes and watched the red sun sinking behind the stackyard trees and the rooks flying back to their nests, Sam outlined the plan for tomorrow.

It was to be the last field to be sown. Listening to him made it all sound simple.

'We'll *nip* into that old Dumpling Field.'

'We'll just have a *snap* for breakfast.'

'Then we'll *whip* that old barley in.'

Had his grandfather not told him years ago: 'If you once get behind you'll always be behind,' and did he not say: 'Drive your work, my boy, and never let your work drive you'?

71

So we drove the work. But for some slight miscalculation in the amounts of seed barley and potatoes we had allowed for the meadow, even the last quarter-acre would have been sown. But that problem now remained.

One more bushel of seed barley or a few bags of seed potatoes would have solved it. Or we might even try some linseed; or a small plot of maize.

Then it was that Old Nart made his suggestion: 'Why not grow some tobacco?' he asked.

Well, what a good idea. It transpired that he had an old pensioner friend in a nearby village who grew some every year for himself and might well be able to let us have the plants.

We puffed at our pipes. The boy George rolled a cigarette. It would help all of us, a kind of grow-it-yourself effort. It would be better than using the coltsfoot that grew in such abundance on Clay Hill. Even Sam, who always declares that he can give up smoking at any time if he likes, though he never does, seemed to brighten up at the suggestion.

We discussed the dibbling-out of the tobacco plants and the curing of the tobacco. And while we were talking Old Nart fumbled for his pouch and filled his pipe, lit up and puffed away, darkening the stable in clouds of black and pungent smoke.

It made even old Captain turn round from his manger to lay back his ears and snort and sniff.

'What's that you're smoking?' asked Sam suspiciously.

Then it came out. It was some of that home-grown baccy his friend had given Old Nart as a birthday present.

☆

THE next morning I saw Sam with Captain and Honey harnessed to the double-breasted plough baulking up the quarter-acre in the meadow.

They were getting ready to sow a few more potatoes.

# APRIL

*When Sam sees the cowslips brighten the banks of the Dumpling Field with golden-tipped flowers all he does is to slip indoors and put on a fourth waistcoat.*

*He knows something. This morning he and Old Nart loaded up the potato planter with the seed and now I see them climbing into it to sit side by side like two old pals in a char-a-banc.*

*The planting goes well; the machine drops two rows of potatoes and covers them with earth in one operation. What a pleasing sight with this April sun shining.*

*Then the sky darkens. As I take shelter I see Sam and Old Nart scramble out of the machine and rush for the ditch in a roaring storm of hailstones. It always happens when the cowslips come.*

# Patch of gold

EVEN THE cowslips in the grass seem to be winking at each other as Old Ben takes me by the arm and leads me down his lane.

'What we want,' he says, 'is Brighter Farming.'

Isn't it bright enough? A lark is singing. The hedges are coming into bud. The barley is a vivid green and there are now young birds in the blackbird's nest in the stackyard. The sky is a brilliant blue. My sows are out cropping the grass to such purpose that my bills for feeding-stuffs should remain stationary (as accounts rendered) for months to come.

'Let's put a little more colour into it,' adds Old Ben as we turn the corner. He smiles as he sees me staring ahead. 'Say it with flowers,' he laughs.

☆

A YEAR ago we had wondered what he was doing when he ploughed up the wide wasted grass verges on both sides of his lane. Perhaps, we thought, he was growing some potatoes for his pigs, or a little additional wheat for his hens, or some fodder beet for his old cow Buttercup. But this is quite unexpected.

For I am as astounded as the poet to see suddenly in front of me, fluttering and dancing in the breeze, a host of golden daffodils!

What can have come over Old Ben? Two theories occur to me. He may have become sentimental, or even slightly religious, in his old age, or this may be a symptom of something much more serious.

Yet we must give Ben the credit for brightening this lane. At the worst it seems a harmless form of lunacy. At the

74

best, unlikely though it is, there may be a complete change of heart.

We haven't long to wait. The next morning we see Ben, his wife and his man Walter all busily engaged there, and a lorry piled high with cardboard boxes turns down the lane.

Later we learn the truth. Old Ben has sent away to London more than 100,000 blooms at sevenpence a bunch of a dozen, which everybody at the Shepherd & Dog agrees is a small fortune.

So now we understand why Old Ben's heart with pleasure fills when he glances at his daffodils.

# Ben's lapse

WHEN OLD Ben offered me a lift home from market in his old lorry the other day I accepted in the right spirit, though I knew what it meant. He wanted someone to help him unload.

I know what these market days are. Neither Ben nor I go very frequently. So that when we do there is usually a mad rush to get things done in time to meet the missus under the town hall clock.

Evidently Old Ben had had a good day. As we droned along past the blaze of blackthorn in the hedges the old lorry creaked and groaned under the weight of its bargains.

Trust him to buy things, whether he really needs them or not. Now and again I could hear the squeal of pigs behind me, and the moo of a calf, and something that rattled like old tin cans.

☆

'You've got a load today,' I said, when I could make myself heard.

'Yes,' mused Old Ben. 'Bought a nice bunch o' blue-and-white pigs. And had a bit o' luck—managed to get three o' them old automatic self-feeders, same as you've got.'

What luck, indeed! I began to think of an excuse to get off before Old Ben reached his farm, knowing how heavy and awkward to handle they were.

But Old Ben went on talking. 'A rare nice calf, too. And I bought some coils of that old wire for electric fencing. Yet I've got an idea I've left something behind. Can't think what it is.'

'You've got enough now,' I told him as the lorry springs seemed to crack under the strain. But I tried to refresh his memory.

'Sugarbeet hoes, perhaps?' I suggested. 'Cartridges for those old pigeons? Mangold seed? A new knife for the mower? Pig minerals or turkey pellets?'

'No, none o' them,' nodded Old Ben. 'Well, there it is, I shall have to get it next time, if I can remember it.'

He had forgotten about it when we turned down his lane. There was enough to think about, anyhow. Farming is such a complex business nowadays. But I was pleased to see his man Walter at the farm when we arrived.

It made the unloading a lot easier, and when we had finished and had got the pigs, even the elusive one, into their sty, Ben smiled at us both and said: 'Now what about a nice glass of home-brewed?'

'I'm still sure I've forgotten something,' he told his man Walter as we went into the kitchen. Then suddenly he clapped his hand to his head.

'Why, what's the matter?' asked Walter, looking anxious.

Old Ben seemed terror-stricken. 'The missus!' he gasped.

# Man with the hoe

THE OTHER day a man came sauntering down the lane. Seeing him reminded me of the dairy farmer who had some trouble with his milk.

One day a smart young woman inspector called at the farm. 'I expect you know why I've come,' she began.

'Yes, I know,' said the farmer. 'You thought I was lonely.'

The lonely days are over now; the snow has gone, the hawthorn blooms all along the hedges, and still nobody comes down our lane apart from this one solitary visitor. But it seemed to us from the way he halted now and then to look over each hedge in turn, as if weighing up the prospects of each crop, that this man might be one of the men who know something about the job. He went straight to the sugarbeet field where Sam was hoeing and stood there watching him. Bless me if it wasn't my old friend Jimmy Daniels from Norfolk.

He stood there thoroughly enjoying himself, spending a holiday in just the way he had always looked forward to spending it, watching someone else doing the work he had done himself, man and boy, on one root crop or another, for the past sixty years.

☆

WE ploughed this field before the snow came, and its furrows were ice-bound through the winter, so that they

77

crumbled into a fine tilth when we sowed the sugarbeet. To make sure of a good plant we put on the full regulation seeding of 15lb to the acre. After all, some of it might rot or fall on stony ground. In the event it all came up with a lot of other things as well. It gave us a lot of hoeing to do.

Sam and I are now doing it. Now and again I have to straighten and stretch myself to ease an aching back. Jimmy smiles: every picture tells a story. 'You ought to be thankful,' he says; 'you've got a good plant.'

I am thankful, not only for this crop, but for the lessons that Jimmy—the foreman when I was a pupil on a Norfolk farm many years ago—taught me. One was a lesson in ploughing, on the first day that I ever put hand to a plough.

Everything went well with two old horses and a single-furrow plough, with Jimmy going up and down the field to give me a start, and I began to think I was a born plough-man. Until lunchtime came and Jimmy sent me back to the stable for a plough-line.

On my return I put my hand to the plough again but it was a different plough; it jumped up and down and in and out of the furrow as if bewitched; the horses started to trot and then went so fast that I had to hold on like grim death while the plough drew a fantastic twisting furrow like the trail of a snake across the field. I was no ploughman after all.

'That's the way to learn,' said Jimmy. Yes, I had learned a lesson—never try to plough when somebody behind my back had taken the share off, and never trust a simple farm worker with an open honest face and twinkling blue eyes.

Sam summed him up despite the disguise of shiny buskins and new hat and brushed suit. 'There's another hoe over there in the hedge,' he said, waving a hand casually in that direction. It was a well-meant invitation, but Jimmy laughed. 'I left one at home,' he said, 'and I don't suppose anybody'll be using that while I'm away.'

Well, it seems Sam was right when he first saw Jimmy coming down the lane. Evidently here is a man who knows something about the job.

# How to make friends

AT LAST I have discoverd the secret of Old Ben's success in life.

He has always had the knack of getting things done. No matter what he has put his hand to, buying pigs or serving on the district council, he has always made a good job of it, to the satisfaction of everybody including himself.

I think he let me into the secret unwittingly while we were sipping his elderberry wine.

He was telling me how, when he was a boy, he sometimes went to see an old retired auctioneer who gave him some tips—three golden rules, in fact—about how to make farming friends and influence country people.

They were:

Please the womenfolk when you go on a farm by going into the house *before* you start tramping round the yard *(remember the mud and the carpets!)*.
Admire the baby.
Mistake the farmer's wife for his daughter.

Of course! I saw it all in a flash. Only the other day he had come to see me. Like so many at this time of the year, I was hoeing sugarbeet. I wondered what he had come for. Was it to buy my pigs, for which I should be profoundly thankful, or my vote, for which I still have a fixed price and an assured market?

☆

ANYHOW, it was an excuse to leave off hoeing. I readily accompanied him to my farmhouse. His boots were shining and spotless as he set his feet carefully on the drawing-room carpet. How greatly he admired my granddaughter Caroline Louise.

I noted how pleased my wife looked after his few opening remarks to her. No wonder we gave him our votes and almost gave him our pigs.

# Pigs for the brigadier

THE SUN has made us all a lot more cheerful. In a few days it changed the face of the farm.

But something more than normal sunshine is needed to explain the extreme hilarity of Sam and Old Nart. The fact is that one of Sam's fondest dreams, something that he's been waiting for ever since his Home Guard days, has come true.

We had advertised some young pigs for sale, and on the telephone a voice informed me that its owner would come down to have a look at them.

He turned up, a portly gentleman with a friendly, rosy countenance and a military bearing which told me that Sam's whispered 'one o' them old army blokes' was probably correct.

Seeing my visitor (it transpired he was a retired Brigadier) reminded ex-Home Guard Sam of much toil and sweat running over fields and crawling through hedges and ditches.

☆

SELLING the pigs was simple. All we had to do was to

persuade the young porkers to stand at attention while they were being weighed. All went well until the Brigadier left a pigsty door open, and the weighed pigs took a short cut to rejoin their mothers in the paddock.

In the wild chase that followed the Brigadier played a worthy, though by no means a leading part. The pigs led by lengths. All his bellowed commands to halt had no effect. With a face like the sunset he ran panting in pursuit.

As Sam said afterwards, it was like old times again. The only difference was that Sam stood and watched with a broad grin while his superior officer did the legwork.

# Story of Charley's dance

CHARLEY CROWE'S three-acre pightle, part of his small farm, seems destined to play the part of a field at Waterloo in village history.

It was grass until the subsidy induced him to plough it up last autumn, and so for years past it has served as a grazing ground for some of his old sows. They grazed there, after the manner of their kind, just long enough to find a hole in the hedge, and almost invariably the holes they found led straight into Old Nart's adjoining garden.

Of course such misfortunes are the common lot of countrymen, and happily we have the knack of being able to laugh at them. Loud squeals and thwacks and curses from the direction of the three acres, particularly at that time of the year when the peas were fit to pick and the cabbages in good heart, were an unfailing source of merriment. In recent years, whenever everybody looked specially cheerful in the Shepherd & Dog, my first guess was that Old Nart's garden had once again been the scene of a successful invasion by Charley's jet-propelled pigs.

81

BUT all is changed now that the three-acre pightle has been ploughed.

Walk down the pleasant lane to Old Nart's cottage, where the green verges on both sides are dotted with cowslips and dandelions, and you find peace, perfect peace. That's what it looks like.

Then suddenly I hear a loud yell from the pightle. I clamber over the hedge.

Charley is there, behaving like a madman, seemingly fighting the air with his fists. He has unhooked the two horses from his drill and abandoned it in the middle of the field. They kick up their heels and break away from him. He is running to the gateway.

I watch him disappearing after the horses down the lane. What can have happened? A strange silence reigns over the three acres. All round it the crops are growing green but it remains unsown.

'He'll have to fallow it instead of cropping it this year,' says a voice behind me, with a chuckle. I turn to find a cheerful, beckoning Old Nart greeting me from his garden. 'Come in and have a look round,' he says.

The lettuces look well. The peas and beans are coming up. The cabbages prosper. And the old man leads me proudly to the bottom of the garden. He hands me a black gauze mask. 'You'd better put it on,' he advises. 'They're some o' them old vicious ones.'

In one corner, facing out to Charley's pightle, are four brand new bee-hives, buzzing with black bees.

# MAY

Old Nart makes his way slowly to the bottom of the Dumpling Field, where a tall ash and a mighty oak stand side by side, as if planted there for his use as a prophet, to tell us what the harvest weather is going to be.

We all know the rhymes—the oak before the ash and we're sure to have a splash; the ash before the oak and we'll have a soak.

One glance—the oak is green, the ash is bare—and Old Nart gives his verdict, a hot summer and a dry harvest.

Old Ben down the lane uses rather different rhymes. For him the oak out before the ash 'fills the farmers' pockets full of cash', while the ash before the oak 'makes the old farmers begin to croak'.

'Give him the money; give us the sunshine,' says Old Nart.

# Happy though hoeing

CHARLEY CROWE pointed to the wild roses in bloom on the hedge. 'There's an old pheasant under that bush,' he said, 'sitting on eleven eggs.'

Would you like to meet a man who enjoys life? Then do as I was rash enough to do the other day, and offer to give Charley Crowe a hand hoeing his surgarbeet. A back-aching job? Yes—and an unrewarding one. I knew there were no dividends in it, as we have not got round to dividend-stripping in our village yet.

I might get 'a mess of peas' or even the promise of a pheasant in due season, but certainly no money. That is the last thing Charley parts with.

Yet in his company the time passed much more quickly than one would expect. Perhaps it is because he knows so much about everything that goes on in the fields. It is such knowledge that brings him 'perks' occasionally—a rabbit or the like—to help eke out the diminishing returns from his small farm.

Now and again we followed the time-honoured custom of leaning on our hoes and 'having a jow', which means that I listened while he talked. Once when doing so we heard an unusual noise in the lane. It was a mere clink-clink, but distinct enough in such quiet to make us peer through the hedge, where we saw an unusual sight.

Half-hidden under the grass that overlapped the road-side, a stoat was pushing a pheasant's egg along with his paws and chasing after it. Then both disappeared down a gully into the ditch.

A trivial incident, but it kept Charley talking as he hoed, until it was time to go home to a farm supper and a farmer's sleep.

Yesterday when I went to Town and walked down Whitehall, I wondered if anyone in the crowds there was half as happy as Charley Crowe.

# There's quite an air about young George

DOWN OLD BEN's green lane, now dotted with cowslips, came the first big lorry-load of skim milk the other day. It was from the Milk Board creamery.

A splendid idea. The Board had too much milk. The surplus, over and above what it could sell in the liquid milk market, had to be converted into cream, and this left thousands of gallons of skim milk to be disposed of every day.

What could be better than to let Old Ben's pigs make pigs of themselves on some of it. 'They'll feel a lot better if they drink more milk,' said Ben, quoting the Milk Board advertisement and omitting to mention his share of the benefits of the experiment. Skim milk has many virtues. A gallon of it is equal to quite a lot of expensive pig-meal, and is much cheaper. It makes good dairy-fed pork and better bacon. Pigs get permanent benefit from it.

The only thing more permanent about it is the smell you get on your clothes.

☆

THAT is where the boy George comes in. His job is to 'slop the hogs' with the skim milk. Unfortunately they slop a lot of it over him. Spare a thought for him whenever you are

85

laying on the butter or being lavish with the cream. For there is a seamy as well as a creamy side to this surplus milk business.

It has nearly caused a riot in the village. Nowadays, when the boy George, after doing his feeding, arrives at the Shepherd & Dog, we all sit up and take notice.

Old Nart hastens to light a pipe of his strongest shag. The landlord looks round for his Home Guard gasmask. Everybody politely makes room for George.

'When you go courting,' Sam warns him, 'she'll think she's walking beside an old badger.'

It's as bad when he gets home. There is a loud yell from the kitchen: 'Take off those ruddy overalls before you come in here!'

No wonder everybody in the village, with the possible exception of Old Ben echoes the Milk Board's advertising slogan with great fervour. We are looking forward to the day when there is no surplus to be skimmed and fed to Ben's pigs. In the Shepherd & Dog in particular we shall certainly all feel a lot better when you people drink more milk.

# A matter of colour

In the Shepherd & Dog, strange as it may seem, we were all talking about the colour bar. We take it very seriously just now. We realise its importance. Most of us don't like racial distinctions of any kind, but some are on one side, and some another.

Yet it would be wrong to say there are two schools of thought. There are several.

Sam, as you might expect, is all for the blacks. In the eyes of my town friend Herbert the whites can do no wrong. Old Ben can argue both ways, as usual, and Old Nart favours a compromise.

I find them all there when I arrive. Just as the blooming of the blackthorn is always followed by a spell of cold weather, so each long day we now have at hoeing the sugarbeet is invariably followed by a spell of relaxation in this bar parlour.

☆

Tonight the colour-bar debate is in full spate. Even Major Tutt, who has spent a lot of time in Central Africa, takes a hand in it.

'Dammit, keep 'em separate,' he booms. 'Why go in for all this cross-breeding?'

Old Nart dissents. 'Some of the best I ever knew were cross-bred,' he ventures.

Sam, going straight to the point, asks: 'Do you want to do away with the old blacks altogether?'

Here Old Ben intervenes. 'Surely we don't want all blacks or all whites. What's wrong with a mixture—blacks and whites?'

There is a loud snort from Herbert. 'It isn't what you

want that matters. It's what the people want.'

'Well, anyhow, I'm all for the blacks,' declares Sam, and turns to Old Nart. 'What do you think about it?'

Old Nart ponders the question. 'I've studied it for a long time,' he begins. 'Let me see, it must be seventy-one years come next muck-spreadin' time since I first thought about it. And I'll tell you what I think. I favour neither the blacks nor the whites. Nor your black-and-whites,' he says, looking at Old Ben.

He pauses and we wait for the verdict. 'Give me the good old blue-and-whites every time.'

Exactly. I agree wholeheartedly. They are just the pigs I keep myself.

# Marry in haste

I KNOW the difference pigs make to a village. They bring in much of our money. When the pig trade is good, we are happy. When it goes down we, too, suffer from depression. And when we talk about gilts, as we often do, we don't mean gilt-edged securities, we mean young sows that have just had or are about to have their first litter of piglets.

But I must confess that until I took the new parson out for a ride the other day, I didn't realise myself how much pigs rule even the most important events of our village life. He is more accustomed to sheep and goats, of course. He doesn't know much about pigs, but he'll learn if he stays long in this neighbourhood. I try to give him a few tips as we travel the lanes.

Cats look down on you, dogs look up to you, but pigs is equal, I explain. You can't make a silk purse out of a sow's ear, I tell him, but you can sometimes fill that purse by selling the progeny from a good sow.

☆

THE road we now follow is fringed with dandelions and cowslips, a reminder that I must soon be making wine. 'Who lives there?' I am asked of a holding where the pigsties preponderate even more than usual.

'The Boy F.,' I reply, using his nickname. 'F for Freddie.' Then I tell my companion all I know about F's history . . . of his enthusiasm for pigs . . . and how keen he is on building up a herd of sows as the mainstay of his farm.

The minister nods. 'Oh, yes, I know him. He wants me to publish his banns as soon as I can. He's rather in a hurry.'

I raise my eyebrows. 'In a hurry?' I query. 'It can't be for income tax, it's too late for that.'

The minister laughs. 'No, he tells me he wants to get married *before his sows pig*!'


# Journey's end

THE OLD harvest waggon has at last come to its journey's end.

For years it has stood idle in the cartshed, made redundant, like its old comrade the horse, by the combine-harvester and the tractor-trailer.

And lately all the other farming items, nowadays in as little demand as itself, have been dumped into it, including Old Nart's scythe, my old fiddle for sowing the clover, spare hoes for town visitors and hay forks for volunteers, followed—during an exasperatingly wet harvest—by Sam's old straw hat.

Yet there is something about it that endures. Its red and blue paint (the old school tie colours for farm implements from time immemorial) is still bright; its stout timbers, that once carried swaying and sometimes toppling loads of sheaves, are still sound. And it links us with happy memories of the past. Many a farmer's boy learned his loading on it, to keep the corners of the load well out, to pack sheaves under his feet, and keep the middle full.

Through many a harvest the veteran horses Captain and Old Don were its faithful companions. And Old Nart can even remember the days, once a year, when it conveyed the parson with a record attendance of Sunday School children to the seaside.

It has outlasted many of them. But yesterday, when we saw the first swallows come to the farm, it was time for the old waggon to go.

☆

SAM took it on its last journey. He fixed it behind the little tractor, the Flying Flea, and careered with it over the fields to Clay Hill at a speed that would have flabbergasted its maker.

There, on the same acres where in its prime it held proud cargoes of corn and heard the call of the 'Hold-ye Boy!' echoing over the stubble, it now stands as a monument to the past as part of Sam's old shruff shed housing the sows now grazing the lucerne.

Fortunately it is as solid as a rock, like its character and reputation. For last night, when the gale blew and the skies opened, many of the other ingredients of the shed—the torn sackcloth, the straw bales, the corrugated iron—were scattered over the field.

But this morning the sows were still sleeping snugly under the old waggon. Alone it had weathered the storm. It was like an old-age pensioner, often forgotten (as on Budget Day), but still stout of heart.

# Armchair farming

How TIMES have changed on the farm! I can remember, and it doesn't seem very long ago, when Sam used to stagger into the Shepherd & Dog at this time of year and sink exhausted into his corner pew on the old oak settle. 'Pint,' he would gasp, and the landlord would hurry to get it, and my town friend Herbert would look respectfully in his direction, and say: 'Drink it up and have another. You've earned it today, I'll warrant.'

Old Nart would sympathise, too. 'Rest yourself,' he'd say, adding a homely phrase: 'Take the weight off the wheels.'

And Sam would mop his brow and mutter: 'Must ha' done about seven acres; properly knocked up old Captain, and the boy George.' I could picture what had happened, with the boy leading the horse, and the flies buzzing round, and Sam toiling behind and hanging on like grim death to the handles of the antique horse-hoe as it churned and swayed its way, mile after mile, through the long rows of sugarbeet.

BUT how different nowadays. When I look over the hedge this morning the boy George is seated on a smart little tractor that purrs smoothly along pulling a grey-painted set of hoes. Perched on top of them, guiding the contraption casually with a lever, sits Sam. There are no flies on either of them. The boy George whistles as he rides. Sam looks as cheerful as the Queen of Tonga.

They move through the sugarbeet without effort. As they reach the end of the rows and turn on the headlands, the boy George moves another lever and up go the hoes and Sam with them. He is suddenly suspended in mid-air, like an unsuspecting visitor on the 'octopus' at a funfair, and just as surprisingly, when the tractor starts on the next journey down the field, he comes down to earth. Another four rows have been hoed. It is as simple as that. The new hoes have everything except a mantelpiece for Sam to put his feet on.

In their wake the weeds wilt and the acres melt away, and when the job is done it makes quite a pleasant change for

Sam to stretch his legs and take a walk down to the Shepherd & Dog.

It is crowded. Nobody makes room for him on the settle these days. We treat him with the quiet tolerance reserved for all such sedentary workers. 'Let him stand,' says Old Nart. 'He's been doin' nothing but sit all day!'

# When a horse is lonely

OF ALL the signs of summer, like the lilac in bloom and the moorhen nesting in the horse-pond, none has been so taken for granted on this farm as the sight every year of my mare Honey cantering out to grass with her tail straight up in the air.

Alas, we shall not see it this year.

For some time now Honey, who celebrated her twenty-first birthday this week, has been a pensioner. On occasions she has helped us to cart an odd load of straw or fodder beet, but usually, despite all the customary protests from Old Nart, we have been too busy on tractors to give her a job at all. She has made no objection to that, but sometimes when I have seen her standing there with her head hanging low I have thought she was lonely. The big horseyard, of which she now has only one small corner, must be peopled in her memory with the shades of her old friends who once lived there—the gentle Princess, the patient Captain, the unforgettable Old Don.

☆

No doubt it was this loneliness that led to her undoing. She forgot all the warnings that the wise Captain had given her against pigs (how often he had snorted and chased them away in this very yard) and made the fatal mistake of fraternising with them.

It went well for a time and Honey formed the habit of stretching her head over the hurdles and rubbing each pig's back in turn with her nose. The pigs liked it so much that they lay in the straw with satisfied grunts and let her carry on indefinitely. When she turned her back on them and started to rub herself on the post in the corner of their pen it was to be expected that they would scratch her back in return, just as old Captain would have done in the old days. This would have been no tale at all if that had happened but the truth is that, in the end, it was Honey who had no tail at all. Unluckily she did not keep her tail up, and as it hung over the hurdle the pigs pulled out every strand of it.

When you read this we shall, for the first time this year, be turning her out to grass. We shall lead her down the lane to the meadow and let her go. She will rejoice in her freedom and the open spaces. She will lift up her head and neigh with delight. She will then kick up her heels and race like a mad horse round the meadow. But she will not lift up her tail.

If old Captain were here I can imagine what he would be saying to her: 'There, didn't I warn you, what did I tell you about pigs? It's heads they win and tails you lose.'

# JUNE

The big advantage of sugarbeet hoeing, if the only one, is that you can 'have a jow' while you hoe.

There is only one rule; never to talk about sugarbeet. So Sam and Old Nart and I talk about hay. At least it offers the prospect of a welcome change of work.

For over the hedge the clover is in crimson bloom. 'When shall we start cutting?' I ask Sam. Not unexpectedly Old Nart interposes with advice handed down by his grandfather.

Apparently the date to remember is the 21st of June.

'Either you cut it and cock it before that day or you don't touch it at all until after,' he warns. 'You always get a lot of rain round about then.'

There is still time. I stretch an aching back. I look at the endless rows of sugarbeet still to be hoed. Yes, tomorrow I think we will cut the hay.

# Hay fever

NEVER HAVE I seen Old Ben look so worried. My first guess is that he may be thinking of the government's policy of complete freedom for farmers. Then I realise it must be the hay.

It is a most exasperating crop in any year. This year it has surpassed itself. The hay harvest has gone haywire.

But what makes this hay problem peculiarly difficult on Ben's farm is the fact that he and his missus are never able to agree about anything connected with it.

'You need experience,' he keeps reminding her. *'A man knows best, my dear.'* He repeats—'Experience.'

It has little effect on Mrs Ben. In all the debates (many of them as heated as the hay) that have taken place recently—on the right time to cut the crop or the doubtful wisdom in this uncertain weather of trying to cut it at all—she has had a lot to say, mainly in opposition.

AND even when the hay was eventually cut on a day of rare June sunshine the arguments still went on.

'We mustn't cock it,' says Old Ben. 'Leave it lying there and with all this sun it'll be fit to cart tomorrow.'

Mrs Ben takes the opposite view. 'It's going to rain,' she declares. 'We *must* cock it.'

She had her way. That evening the hay was put up into big rounded heaps or cocks, safe from the rain if it should rain. But the rain held off.

It was just what Old Ben expected. The next morning the hay was beginning to heat. It had hay fever. It would be fatal to cart it. The heaps would all have to be pulled down and thrown out. The job would have to be started all over

96

again. We have a stock phrase for such happenings. It is: *'Now what you ought to have done. . . .'*

Old Ben knows it now. He should have left the hay uncocked. He looks accusingly at his wife. 'Just what I thought would happen,' he complains.

But that good woman is unperturbed. 'You shouldn't have paid any attention to me,' she says scornfully. 'After all, you always have said that a man knows best.'

As usual, she makes hay of all his arguments, and so far that's the only hay made this year on Old Ben's farm.

# Important people

ANY FLEETING doubts that Sam and I may once have had about our importance in the scheme of things have been finally dispelled by visiting our county agricultural show.

In our village we have been particularly fortunate. The show people selected a site quite close to us. So when Old Nart looked over his hedge the other day and saw all the stands going up not far from his back garden he immediately prophesied that the show could not fail to be a huge success.

'There'll be a rare lot o' people there this year,' he said. 'It'll be nice and handy!'

☆

NATURALLY we all go. And what an education for us! The new machines, the displays of cattle, the parades of horses round the grand ring, the dog show, the flower show, the poultry exhibits, the show of bees (Sam makes a beeline away from them, 'their feet are hot', he says) and the agricultural education exhibition.

What lessons we can learn! But all these are as nothing to what the trade stands have to teach us. Never before did we realise how many good friends we had and how important we were.

Sam's first surprise is to see a smiling portly gentleman with a carnation in his buttonhole welcoming him into a palatial marquee.

'Pleased to see *you*,' he says to Sam, pumping his hand like a marginal candidate. A table is soon spread before him and a charming waitress asks him, 'What can I get you, Sir?'

Sam looks round the marquee crowded with farmers and workers he knows, all busy with large plates of ham and all the beer they can drink.

'Plate of ham and a pint, please,' he says.

Like him, these sharers of the feast are all deserving guests, having lately spent a lot of their time and energy humping numerous hundredweights of the fertilisers sold by this firm and broadcasting them laboriously over the fields. Naturally the friendly gentleman shakes hands again as Sam leaves, saying, 'Pleased you were able to come.'

What a mistake to think, as some seem to do, that these shows have no educational value. We learn such a lot. It surprises us to learn how popular we are, and it probably surprises some of the firms even more to learn what a lot of customers they have.

Along my route to the grand ring there are marquees everywhere. Invited by a man who sells me pig-meal I turn into another of them before the show closes. I am accorded the same welcome that we important people have come to expect.

I recognise a familiar figure sitting in the corner. I hear once again the familiar voice.

'Plate of ham and a pint, please,' Sam is saying.

# Money for ham

ANY BEGINNER in pigs, of course, is bound to have teething troubles.

It was so with my town friend Herbert. Some time ago he tried his hand at buying young pigs (incidentally, from Old Ben) and fattening them for bacon. He found it would be cheaper to buy the bacon. The only profit went to Old Ben. But it gave Herbert an idea. Why not produce young pigs and let somebody else do the fattening? He bought an old sow.

The day came when the sow was due to farrow. It was an anxious day, more so for Herbert than the sow. He spent it pacing up and down outside the sty, and peering through a hole in the wall. Nothing happened. This sow, like most, had a preference for two o'clock in the morning. So that when Herbert, who had fallen asleep sitting on a bag of barley meal in the adjacent mealhouse, woke up he thought he was dreaming when he saw twelve lovely little pigs suckling the old sow.

'Beginner's luck,' said Sam when he saw them a bit later. It seemed like it. They were lively piglets.

Never were there such pigs, thought Herbert. He spent hours watching them grow into money. It looked like money for ham. As they rooted Herbert gloated. Nothing could be more fatal where pigs are concerned.

For the next day he is leaning over the pigsty door in anxious consultation with Sam. The little pigs are squealing. The old sow squats there obstinately. She has had enough.

'It's their teeth,' says Sam, fumbling in his pocket for a pair of pincers.

'Good heavens, surely they haven't got teeth at that age,' says Herbert.

He soon knows better when one of the little pigs bites him while he is opening its mouth to enable Sam to do some dental surgery. With Herbert holding them and Sam cutting their teeth, the piglets are dealt with one by one and put back with their mother. She settles down more comfortably now.

It is just one more trivial incident in the history of the farm; just one of the teething troubles that are likely to happen to anyone pig-headed enough to go in for pigs.

# We're all toffs

OLD NART is talking. It is the time of wild roses. They make such a picture in the hedge outside the Shepherd & Dog that perhaps they account for his taking such a rosy view of things. Not only is this world, according to him, the best of all possible worlds, but also this village of Lesser Snoring is by far the best of all villages to live in.

How does he make that out? We have advantages.

We have a post office where they pay out pensions and even accept telegrams when really necessary.

We have a part-time hairdresser's open on Sunday mornings where we can read the local paper for nothing.

We have a village green with a church in one corner and the Shepherd & Dog in the other.

And (except when featherbed-farmer Ben is using his patent automatic bird-scarers by day and night) we even have peace and quiet on occasions.

YET I should have thought that other villages had similar advantages. Why is Old Nart so enthusiastic about our own?

'I'll tell you,' he says, like an oracle. 'There's one thing about Lesser Snoring that pleases me most of all. It's a Village without Toffs.'

When I look round I realise how right he is. String-tied trousers, battered sunhats, open shirts, just as we've come in from the fields; the schoolmaster, sitting in the corner there, one of us; the parson, poor as a church mouse; not a Toff among us. How times have changed in the village; no wonder the atmosphere is so friendly.

Another voice chimes in. It's my friend Podd the pig-dealer. 'Fill them up,' he says. 'A toast to Lesser Snoring, the village of No Toffs.'

'You're one,' laughs Old Nart, lifting his pint mug.

He proposes an amendment: 'Well, perhaps I'd better say that nowadays we're all Toffs.'

# Sam orders beef

No SOONER had Sam lost his money on the Derby than he looked into old Judy's calving box and saw the result of another gamble. It was a milk-and-beef gamble with the old cow. It began during last harvest.

He remembers well the August days when the corn was ripening and his friend the artificial inseminator came down the lane with a boxful of test-tubes and a wide choice of bulls for Judy.

101

'What'll you have this time?' asked the operator; 'A Jersey or a Guernsey?'

'I think we'll try a Hereford,' said Sam.

If he had said an elephant I hardly think the operator could have been more astonished. 'What, a beef bull on a dairy cow like Judy!' he exclaimed.

It seemed unreasonable at the time, but Sam had been giving this problem some thought. Judy had been a good old cow; she had not only given us a lot of milk, but almost every year for a long time she had produced a heifer calf. How long would this sequence of heifer calves go on? There was the law of averages. It'll be a bull calf next time, thought Sam, so it had better be a beefy one.

☆

MARY, the land-girl, agreed with him. I think Judy did too.

Her heifer calves would naturally make dairy cows, but her bull calves, with all this Jersey blood in them, would merely make meat pies. They would be useless for rearing into big bullocks of beef.

Moreover, Sam had been reading in the paper at that time how all the experts were saying that farmers ought to produce beef as well as milk from their cows. The way to do it (said a certain doctor at Cambridge) was to divide the herd into two groups and mate the better milkers with a dairy bull and the poorer milkers with a beef bull.

To put this plan into action with a one-cow herd like Judy the only thing that Sam could do was to try a beef bull occasionally and hope for the best.

It came this morning. It was as welcome a sight as the first wild rose I had just seen along the hedge in the Dumpling Field. Close beside Judy a strong little red calf with an all-white head was lying in the straw. A little red meat at last! It was a real Hereford bull calf. The old cow has not only given us milk and butter and cheese, and even cream and a calf every year, but she has now given us beef as well.

It was just what the doctor ordered.

# One man's rain

THE PINK and white roses now dotted all along the hedges are not more common than the shocks and surprises that occur nowadays in modern farming. For no sooner had Judy the Jersey cow presented us with a Hereford beef calf, than we looked over the valley to see a haymaking miracle in action on, of all places, Old Ben's farm.

I had a talk with him when I walked down to Clay Hill the other day and we agreed that all the crops would be better for some rain, except the hay. Ben and I had our hay lying out in swathes so we decided to postpone our prayers for rain for a time, however badly the barley needed it.

I went with Sam to have a look at mine. We found it needed turning.

The next job would be to rake it up and heap it up in cocks and then, if the weather held good, to cart it load by load and build it all into a big stack. If it didn't rain I thought we might finish the job in a fortnight.

☆

WE were just in the middle of doing it, and were wondering why Old Ben was still letting his hay lie out and apparently not taking any action, when a lot of unusual noise from his farm made us look in that direction.

A machine that in the distance resembled a red caterpillar was snaking its way round his hayfield. It swallowed the swathes as it went, and there was a long trail behind of tightly compressed oblong bales of hay, that came out like slabs of chocolate from a slot machine. Old Ben with his tractor-trailer was there, picking up the bales as fast as they fell, and taking them away into his barn. In no time, it seemed, the field was clear.

We went on laboriously turning the hay. 'If it doesn't rain, and the old forecast says it won't, we shall cock it tomorrow,' said Sam.

The outlook seemed good. Old Ben, as I expected, was all smiles when he came down the lane a little later. 'We *want* some rain *now*,' he said.

He was smiling still more when I met him in the Shepherd & Dog that evening, and the sky had opened and the rain was pouring down in torrents. 'This'll do more good than we shall,' he observed, rubbing his hands. 'This rain is just what we wanted.' As he raised his glass he gave me a special wink and a smile.

# Pigsty alibi

IT WAS quite a good idea when Sam supplied the pigs he was fattening in his back garden with a self-feeder. It was a home-made affair, with several compartments from which the pigs helped themselves to dry meal by pushing up tin lids with their snouts. It had the great advantage that Sam could fill up the hopper with a hundredweight of meal on a Saturday morning and then forget about them for the weekend.

Such an idea was, of course, in keeping with the present-day trend of mechanising everything on the farm. If it had any disadvantage it was merely that the pigs, in their natural desire to make full use of this new self-help service, made so much noise—especially at night when Sam was trying to get to sleep—banging the lids up and down.

Even this, however, proved to have its uses on occasions. There was last Thursday evening, for example, when Sam went, somewhat surreptitiously, to the speedway.

Only that morning Old Nart had delivered a strong

lecture in the stable against such a deadly sin. 'Speedway!' he snorted with disgust; 'Where should I be if I fooled my time away on things like that?' He looked at Sam and the boy George with such a piercing eye that both of them (although they had tickets in their pockets) decided it was wiser not to argue.

☆

No doubt, too, they felt guilty. There were so many jobs left undone that they ought to have done. There was the garden. There were Sam's pigs, too. For so many generations of village life has this sense of sin been inculcated that we always steal away as silently as the Arabs when we visit sporting events at a time when we ought to be in the Dumpling Field or the garden.

With Old Nart's condemnation still ringing in his ears, Sam slipped away. It is difficult to believe that he could have enjoyed himself. He certainly ought not to have done. But by far the worst part of the business was to meet Old Nart's eye next morning.

The job then was second-hoeing the sugarbeet. It provided a rare opportunity for a cross-examination. But, to Sam's relief and surprise, Old Nart was in a more than usually friendly mood.

'I came down your lane last night,' he said to Sam as they hoed away side by side. 'I heard you banging away there in your old pigsty.'

# JULY

*Come harvest we may have a new crop, of which Old Nart and I are both substantial consumers.*

*We believe in self-sufficiency. For breakfast we grow our own bacon and eggs and mushrooms; for the mid-day meal a good wheat for bread-making. The milk from Buttercup makes cheese and butter, and our barley is a malting sample for beer. So only one thing is lacking.*

*'Pass the pickled onions,' I say as we sit in the Shepherd & Dog. Old Nart's mouth and eyes water when I mention the pickling onions harvest we shall soon be reaping ourselves.*

*He knows his onions, you see. You may, too, if you give us a hand. If you have tears, prepare to shed them then.*

# Keeping up with the milk!

I HAVE often heard Ben say that you've got to keep moving in farming, and when I saw him milking his old cow Buttercup on the meadow the other evening I began to understand what he meant.

He sold his old farm and herd of cows some time ago, and when he saw all the good companions he had lived with for years come under the hammer and then leave the farm that had always been their home he had sad afterthoughts. He missed the monthly milk cheque and the weekly pound of butter.

Unable to do anything about the cheque, he solved the butter problem by buying old Buttercup. She was a good cow. And anybody who passes through the village on any of these summer evenings when the corn is ripening will see Ben milking her on his meadow near the green.

There was hardly any alternative. The new farm had no cowhouse, and Ben certainly had no intention of spending his money on building one. So twice a day now you can almost set your clock by the regularity with which Ben walks down the lane with his stool and pail and sidles up to the old cow.

☆

IT may seem a trivial episode, but it is part of our village life and everybody knows about it. It is sufficiently interesting for people like Old Nart to walk that way at the appointed hour, and occasionally even my town friend Herbert will cycle down to the green.

For although Buttercup is a placid old cow and a splendid milker with many virtues, she has one little fault. Like that little old black'un you always get in a bunch of pigs you're trying to count, she never will stand still for long.

So we watch Ben settle himself down on his stool after saying: 'Whoa, old girl,' get his pail in position, start by squirting the first streams of milk on each hand in turn and get ready to milk.

Then the old cow, after looking round to make quite sure that Ben has made himself comfortable, will stop grazing and move forward a few paces, leaving her would-be milker crouching over a pail like a seasick sailor.

It amuses Old Nart, but when Ben finally manages to complete the job the old man is the first to offer congratulations. 'You've got to keep up with everything in farming these days,' he tells Ben.

# Roses round the door

IT SEEMS such an incredible story that anyone might think Old Nart invented it. Who would believe that townspeople like Bill and his wife from Chiswick should so take things for granted that they bought their country cottage without . . . but I anticipate.

They did buy it. They became next-door neighbours to Old Nart. They loved the place. (Of course, there were roses round the door.) They were temporarily in the seventh heaven of delight. It was such a treat for them to leave the crowds and the smoke and be able to look over open fields where the corn is beginning to turn golden in the sunshine.

I can understand them. All round us the crops are now ripening into harvest. Along the winding lanes the roses and the rest-harrow are in bloom. Scents of hay and sweetbriar, and wild mint crushed under your feet, come to you on a stroll over the meadows. It is just the time of year to come into the country.

☆

OLD NART was the first to welcome them. 'How d'you think you'll like it?' he asked. 'It's grand,' said Bill. 'Just the place we've been looking for.'

They stood there happily, having just finished putting their odds and ends of furniture into place. Then Bill had an inspiration. 'How about a cuppa?' he asked his wife. 'Just the job,' she agreed. 'I'll get one straight away.' She went into the kitchen to fill the kettle.

'Can't find a tap,' she shouted presently. Bill looked at Old Nart. 'Perhaps our neighbour here will show you where it is,' he suggested.

Old Nart laughed. He'd often heard that one-half of the world doesn't know how the other half lives. *'A tap! You'll have to go across the road to the pond. There aren't any taps round here.'*

# A perfect cow

A FRIEND of mine in the town whose son wants to learn farming took the boy with him the other day and went to seek advice on the matter from a very shrewd old farmer.

The farmer considered the problem gravely. Then he looked at the boy and said—*'He won't live long enough!'*

That's the drawback. Nobody realises it now better than Major Tutt. Ever since he started farming a few years ago he has been learning and, like the rest of us, still has a lot to learn.

One of his recent lessons, which has incidentally provided us with a little light relief, has been to learn that farmers as a class are seldom given to exaggeration. We are modest in our claims, both for our crops and livestock. If we have to make an estimate it is usually a conservative one.

For example, you never hear Old Ben, even in his most boastful mood, talk about a bumper crop. He leaves that to the newspapers. When we look over the gate, as we are doing now, at golden-brown fields of waving wheat, we never hint at record yields. The most that Old Nart or anyone else ventures to say is—'Well, very likely that'll be half-tidy.'

It is the same when an old sow has averaged ten pigs a litter twice a year for about ten years. 'Not a bad old sow, Susan,' says Sam. 'When she goes for sausages she won't owe you a lot.'

☆

IT was possibly this gift of understatement which misled my neighbour Major Tutt.

To keep up his milk contract he had to go to market a few days ago to look round for another cow and there he happened on Old Ben. That worthy was immediately helpful. He led the way to where his old cow Buttercup, her udder bulging with milk, was waiting to be sold in the ring.

Obviously she was a milker and Ben could quite properly give her a character as such. 'Well, what's wrong with her?' asked the Major.

'Nothing at all,' said Ben. 'Nothing worth mentioning. There's only one thing, that when you milk her she's a bit inclined to lift one of her hind feet a trifle.'

The auctioneer failed to mention even that trifling fault. 'Look at her milk vein,' he implored everybody. 'There's a milker for you, gentlemen.'

Major Tutt bought her reasonably enough and when he got her back to his farm nobody could find any fault with her and everybody said he'd got a bargain. Nor could he find any fault himself until he went to milk her and measured his length in the cowhouse gutter. She was almost, as he observed afterwards, 'a perfect cow'.

The only drawback is that she lifts her foot a bit when you milk her.

# Old Nart's day off

OLD NART'S working plans for the day are always made plain by signs he makes outside my window when I am having my breakfast.

He uses a form of agricultural semaphore. Sometimes I see him going through the motions of swinging an imaginary scythe, or sometimes he chops away as if using a hoe, and usually this is followed by his pointing in the direction of the job. So when the other morning he came as usual and gave me a thumbs-up sign and then imitated the riding of a jockey at full gallop I guessed he intended having a day off to go to the point-to-point races in the next village.

As a casual worker (sometimes too much so in my opinion) he can leave off when he likes and is the only one on this farm who can afford a day off at this time of the year. But I gave him a cheery wave and my blessing. I had heard that he had been making a special study of the form of local horses all through the winter and that, from the information he had gained, he fancied a horse known as Poor Sailor.

☆

I HEARD the full story the next morning. He found everybody most friendly. But, strangely enough, nobody thought much of Poor Sailor, and everybody said that Holdfast could not fail to win. Horsey people swore by Holdfast. Then Old Nart met a benevolent gentleman who handed him, for five shillings, an envelope containing a sure tip for a winner. It was Holdfast again. 'Holdfast's the horse,' another friend told him. 'Old Harry says so, and he's tipped three winners today already.'

A little reluctantly, Old Nart put his money on Holdfast. For one thing it reminded him of the variety of wheat, of the same name, that we were growing on the Dumpling Field.

Later on it reminded him even more of what the bookie did with the money. Poor Sailor won, of course.

Then Old Nart met with even more friendly people who tried to show him how simple it was to 'find the lady' out of three cards placed face downwards on a folding camp stool. It seemed a lot easier than hoeing sugarbeet. When finally

113

he put his money on the chosen card all I need add is that the only lady he found anywhere that day was the one waiting impatiently and with a lot to say when he got home.

He is the only man on this farm who can afford to take a day off, and now even he cannot afford to do it again.

# Ben gets his price

WHEN MR Podd the pig-dealer came down the lane the other evening to look at the pigs Old Ben had to sell, events followed the course that can be expected whenever two very simple countrymen meet to make a deal.

On no account, to begin with, is there any mention at all of pigs. The dealer asks after Ben's health, and that of his family, and then they walk round the yard, keeping well away from the pigs, and discuss harvest prospects, and lean together over the meadow gate, standing and staring at Ben's old cow, Buttercup. For the next half-hour they talk about cows. How Ben has had trouble with Buttercup and had the veterinary surgeon to attend her, and how she had gone off her milk. 'She's getting old,' says Ben, 'and her indigestion's not so good as when she was young.' The pig-buyer nods gravely in sympathy.

Then they look at Ben's car standing in the cartshed. It is not only dilapidated, but also somewhat spattered owing to an old grey owl roosting on a beam above it during the past few weeks. 'Farmers' paint,' is the dealer's comment.

☆

OLD Ben, they say, would sell anything, even his wife, but the price has to be good, and by the time they come to the pigs in their pen he has completed some simple arithmetic.

Taking the figure he first thought of, he adds a crown apiece because they are his pigs; another because they are blue-and-white pigs—favourites in local markets; another because the dealer's coming shows that the trade is going up; another because there is a lot of barley about; and a final one to make sure he has asked enough.

Mr Podd keeps poking the smallest pig and saying what a pity it spoils the sale of the others.

At last he makes a bid. It is prefaced by a eulogy of himself. 'My father was an honest man,' he says, 'and so is his son. I'll give you eight pounds; it's a good price, and I'm biddin' you fair.'

He adds a crown, and then another. Finally, as he is getting into his car, he lifts a horny hand, brings it down like a sledge-hammer on Ben's open palm, and gives him all the money he asks.

Evidently, the pig trade is better than we thought, and anybody who didn't know Ben might expect him to be completely satisfied. But I have never yet known him happy after a pig deal. Either he doesn't get his price, which worries him, or he does get it and thinks he has not asked enough.

# The battle of barley field

ONE ADVANTAGE of growing an early-ripening kind of barley is that you can sometimes rush it on the market before anybody else and make a good price. At least, that was Sam's idea.

This year the early barley promised well. We sowed it on Lower Riding, a field in the valley bordering Old Ben's farm. A week ago, with the sun shining and the butterflies dancing over it, the crop looked as safe as a gilt-edged investment. But we had forgotten the crows.

They came down in a black cloud one morning and

taught us the disadvantage of growing the only early-ripening barley in the district. They had already flattened and devoured half an acre when Sam went down with his gun and frightened them over to Old Ben's farm.

☆

THE next thing we saw was Ben crawling along the ditch with his gun to frighten them back again.

This neighbourly exchange went on with little advantage to either side until Sam brought up his heavy artillery. He fixed up an oil drum in the hedge and suspended in it a patent crow-scarer consisting of cartridges on a slow-burning rope which rocked the field with terrific explosions.

That finished Old Ben for a short time, but it was not long before he had fitted up a similar contraption so that we were all square again. It looked as if we might have to resort either to germ warfare or an atom bomb.

Fortunately, we have been spared that final reckoning. As suddenly as they had come the crows departed. It was a grinning Ben who waved over the hedge to me next morning.

'Old Major Tutt's got some early barley near the wood,' he said. 'All those old crows have gone there.'

We congratulated each other warmly. But we're hoping they'll stay there.

# Sally's farm

MY OLD dog Sally had a good life on the farm. Bless her, it was her farm; she knew every corner of it; every field, every ditch, every rat-track through the spinney, every rabbit-hole in the bank round the Dumpling Field, every path through the meadows.

She lived her life on the good earth, saw the corn sown,

116

the green blades coming up through the soil, the ears ripening to harvest, the stacks going up, the thatchers busy roofing them with straw, the bustle on threshing days, the rats and mice scurrying from the stack bottom.

For what purpose these hedges, thick with hazel and brambles, these fields of waving wheat now changing to red-gold, if not to hide rabbits and leverets and pheasants, and why these grass-grown tracks and quiet winding lanes, if not for hunting walks round the farm?

She waited for me, lying under the shade of the chestnut tree near the horse-pond, whenever I left the farm. Even now, as I write, it seems to me that I see her face at my window again. Her paws on the sill, an appealing look in those brown eyes, that seems to say—'What on earth are you wasting your time there for? Let's go and see if there are any rabbits in the mangolds or amongst the potatoes, or along the ditch down the lane.'

NEVER again, Sally. I shall write, and not see you watching me impatiently through the window, and finish writing and, alas, not find you lying waiting for me on the mat outside the door.

You would have enjoyed these harvest days that are now coming. You always did. I can see you now, on the stubble, in the sunlight, panting, your tongue hanging out, tail wagging, your mouth open in a happy grin, watching the boys with their sticks and the binder cutting the ripe corn, and eagerly waiting for the rabbits.

You walked beside me through the passing years of the war. We shared the meat ration—and sometimes supplemented it, thanks to you. You never grumbled and never criticised, not even my writing the *Country Diary*.

I remember when you had your puppies in the hollow trunk of the elm in the stackyard, and how, that night when it rained in torrents, you carried them one by one into a 'better hole' under the pigsties, for shelter.

117

You came with me when I rolled the oats and harrowed the wheat, or walked in the moonlight of double summer time to shut up the poultry.

I shall always remember.

For now Mary the land girl, your great friend, has covered a grave with flowers in a shady corner of the lawn, and watered it with tears, for Sally lies there.

Harvest has come, but no longer will she walk beside me through the golden land.

The consolation is in the memory of the many happy days my Sally once spent on the farm.

# Cash by the sack

SAM MADE quite a casual remark this morning which even made me forget about the weather.

We were standing in the cartshed watching the rain make bubbles in the horse-pond. The outlook was certainly a bit dismal. But, like the incurable optimists that all farmers always are, we were talking confidently about the coming harvest.

Boasting is a foolish thing to do in farming. Once I heard a farmer brag to another one: 'I'll have you know, mister, that I'm a twelve-thousand-pound man.'

As one might expect in a job like farming, he lived to regret it.

☆

BUT at no time is boasting more foolish than just before harvest. Look at these walls of wheat thick with grain, and the barley already tinged with gold. Tomorrow they may be laid flat, and Sam may have to reach up for his scythe to harvest them.

Yet we have to plan and make due preparations—the combine-harvesting; the labour necessary; the carting and storing and selling of the grain, and that all-important item, the sacks.

Sacks play a big part. On wet mornings on some jobs Sam uses one as an apron and one round each leg. They are useful as mats, as cushions for tractor-seats, and to stop up holes in barns.

When I sold a couple of little pigs the other day they went away in one.

They also serve as a measure of the farm's progress—up or down. When we talk about crops we always think in terms of sacks per acre.

I well remember the first harvest I had on this farm. A friend helped me to cart it with one ancient horse and a tumbril.

We threshed it all out in one day. The total yield—the figure that stays in my mind—was one hundred and one sacks of corn.

It was Sam's remark that stirred up this memory. He was talking, of course, about sacks.

☆

ALL round us the rain was pelting down. There were dark clouds over the Dumpling Field. Old Nart was shaking his head and saying: 'Just look at it—all this rain just when we ought to be starting harvest.'

And then Sam suddenly said: 'D'ye know, you'll want a thousand sacks this year.'

A thousand sacks! It was as if the sun had suddenly come out again. I forgot the rain.

I am crossing my fingers now. The crops look grand. I am sure that Sam has made careful calculations. The barleys are heavy. 'Not one ear could I find with less than fourteen grains a side; that's what you want to look for,' said Sam. But I mustn't boast; anything can happen yet.

I am just left wondering whether, after harvest, I shall be able to say to my neighbour, Old Ben: 'I'll have you know, mister, that I'm a thousand-sack man!'

# AUGUST

*Nothing gives more comfort to a farmer than to see other farmers worse off than he is. So the other day in the middle of harvest—and what a harvest!—I went to see Old Ben.*

*'Look at it,* August, *just when it ought to be hard and dry,' he was saying. We walk in gumboots round the crops.*

*We look at the wheat that will have to be cut with a scythe, the beans with a grass-mower, and the peas that cannot be cut at all.*

*What a problem. I tell Sam about it. He says: 'There always were wet harvests and good harvests. I remember the old farmers moanin' when I was a boy.'*

*'They'll get over it; they always did,' says Sam.*

# Rogues on the land

IT SHOCKED my town friend Herbert to hear we had so many rogues in the wheat field.

How did they get there? Did someone leave the gate open, he wondered? Such things do happen at this time of year, just when the corn is ripe and harvest is about to begin. Worst of all, it was the special new *Petit Quin Quin* wheat which we drilled on High Riding last October with such special care. For convenience on this farm we always referred to it as 'that old petty wheat'.

We handled the seed like diamonds and harrowed it in with a benediction. On the rare occasions when we were not too busy with other crops we walked down to the field to see how it was growing. From thin lines of green, sketched vaguely across the field, it grew into a bumper crop of a million massed golden ears waving in the wind. It was a show field, for this was no ordinary wheat, but a new pedigree variety which we were now growing specially for seed. Farmers from far and near came to see it; everybody admired it.

Except, as often happens, the very people we hoped would admire it, the two seed experts who came specially down the lane just before harvest to look at the crop with a view to buying it for seed.

Sam took them down to the field like an artist about to uncover a masterpiece. There was 'gold in that there field', to judge from his manner and his talk about it.

It was a pity the buyers could not see it as well.

All they could or would see were the few strange different ears of wheat appearing here and there, a little taller than the surrounding crop. 'Rogues,' muttered one of them. 'Yes, looks like Little Joss,' said the other, naming another wheat variety as though referring to a cat burglar, and indeed no burglar could have done more damage to our prospects of gold in the crop.

☆

IT is as plain as a dead sow on a muckheap that something is wrong when Sam comes back from the inspection, and talks to Old Nart about it. 'Too many o' them old rogues,' he explains.

How they got there is a mystery, but it means that we cannot sell the special new wheat for seed after all. Well, we shall have to make it into bread.

But it has taught us all, and my town friend Herbert, another farming lesson. Now we know that there are 'rogues' on the land as in any other way of life, and that they are liable to crop up where and when you do not expect them.

# Holiday harvest

WHEN I went to see Old Ben in hospital, we talked about that greatest of popular illusions called *harvest*.

His doctor had told him he must have his operation without further delay. 'Very well,' Ben had at last agreed, 'I can spare ten days beginning July 31st.'

That was how it was arranged. He looked very cheerful sitting up in bed. I told him that harvest had already begun on some farms, and that some samples of early barleys were already being offered to the merchants.

Then we talked about old times. He could remember when men 'took a harvest' by the acre. They mowed the corn, tied it up, turned it if it was barley, loaded and carted it, and raked behind the loads. They often worked until it was dark, with lanterns hanging beside the waggons; and built it all up into great stacks in the stackyard.

'I can remember once carting beans all night and having supper in the field at midnight when there was a full moon,' said Old Ben.

☆

'WHEN you've finished this job here you'll just about be starting harvest on your own farm,' I reminded him.

Ben nodded. 'Yes, it's all settled,' he said. 'It will all be harvested by the combine. The sacks will be mechanically loaded in the fields. The corn will be dried, if necessary, and automatically weighed and loaded again on lorries and off it will go to the merchants. That's why I arranged to be here just now,' he added with a broad grin.

*'With luck I ought to be home at the right time to have a nice quiet rest and convalescence doing a harvest!'*

I left the ward to the accompaniment of a loud laugh from Old Ben that shattered yet another farming illusion.


# The customers are waiting

SAM HOPES to make all the sacks of barley we produce this year walk off the farm on four legs, if he can. It sounds like a conjuring trick, but there is really no mystery. I saw him preparing for it this morning with the help of Old Nart.

In the next field the combine-harvester was busy in the barley. In many ways it was still the old familiar harvest scene.

There were the inevitable small boys with sticks and with them a buxom land-girl with sleeves rolled up and just as eager as they to get a rabbit. There was the usual group of women, one holding a baby, standing at one end of the field, and the customary man with a dog on a leash and on the alert at the other.

The only difference was that, in place of the chattering binder throwing out sheaves, this big new red machine snorted and swallowed the crop and spewed it out in long swathes of straw and fat sacks of ready-threshed grain.

It looks like good barley. I take a handful out of one of the sacks and beckon to Sam. We agree it is a useful sample. Old Nart, as usual, says it is one of the best he has ever seen. The man driving the combine speaks very highly of it. Everybody seems quite satisfied.

All that remains, in normal times, is to get the buyers to agree.

☆

SOMETIMES that is a little more difficult. They are apt to be critical. Sometimes they hardly seem to know what they want. But it does not matter much this year. For Sam and Old Nart have been busy this morning filling a sheltered yard with fresh clean wheat straw and iron troughs and getting this new home ready for some other esteemed and good customers who know exactly what they want and will be glad to have my barley and swallow it without question or criticism.

They stand now on the other side of the hedge, seeming to watch the combine as interested spectators. They are my old sows Lamplighter and Susan and all their sisters and families of little pigs.

They are waiting to convert the barley into bacon. The idea meets with general approval. Old Nart has only one qualification to make. He hopes for his own sake that somebody else will spare a little barley for the beer.

# Sam finds the easy way...

JUST AT this moment Sam, looking like a modernised Boadicean charioteer, is advancing on his tractor (armed with seven pointed steel prongs in front) towards the Dumpling Field.

He is on his way to Big Smithies, the ten acres where the combine harvester is busy in this sunshine processing drooped ears on yellow straw into fat sackfuls of barley. Even Old Nart, who is watching him, can, like the ranks of Tuscany, scarce forbear to cheer.

Everything was so different in his young days. He can remember the foreman's ribald remarks when he was first taught the correct way to hug a 19-stone sack of beans. He can remember when no man on a farm qualified for a full wage unless he could carry that weight of beans on his back up wooden steps to the granary.

Time was on most farms when those who grunted the loudest were credited with doing the most. Everything, you see, had to be lifted by hand.

Nowadays, the only time we have to lift anything is when we go on a neighbour's farm to borrow something and find he isn't there, or when we go to the Shepherd & Dog after the day's harvesting is done.

The arrival of Sam's seven-pronged mechanical muck-lifter was the beginning of this transformation. As its hydraulic power responded to a flick of his finger it lifted a tumbril-load of farmyard manure with ease.

Then we used it (as we are now doing) for sackfuls of corn. It fulfils all expectations. It gathers them up off the field where the 'combine' has deposited them and places them, four at a time, on the trailer, as neatly and quickly as our old tabby cat picks up fieldmice on a newly-cut stubble.

The climax came when my poor old sow, Susan, dropped dead with a heart attack. According to Sam's estimate, if she weighed a pound she weighed 50 stone. When the plain van came to take her away to some mysterious destination (we hope it was to a cats' home) once again Sam did his now-famous stand-back act. 'Leave it to me,' he said.

126

A few minutes later old Susan, for the first time in her long life, was airborne. Neither the old sow nor anybody else grunted. The mechanical muck-lifter had relieved us of another weighty problem.

# Just like old times

IN THESE days of farming mechanisation it is news if anybody buys a scythe. It becomes a miracle if anybody like my town friend Herbert, who has now settled in the village, buys one.

Yet that is exactly what has happened. When it became known at the Shepherd & Dog, several old farmers there issued cordial invitations to Herbert to try his hand at harvesting their laid barley.

It is hardly necessary to add that these good-will offerings were declined with thanks. But Herbert soon enlightened his hearers. After having tried geese as a means of keeping down the grass in his orchard he had decided to save trouble and expense by mowing it himself.

'Bought one of these new patent all-metal ones,' he explained. 'It's a treat to handle. Ever tried one?'

☆

OF course, most of us have handled scythes, and Old Nart can remember being 'lord of the harvest' and leading the mowers through the corn, but nowadays everybody agrees that the best place for a scythe is to hang it on the old apple tree and let it stay there.

However, this new scythe was apparently something quite different. 'I'm going to mow my orchard with it tomorrow,' Herbert announced casually.

He was just sharpening it when the first caller, the postman, arrived. 'A little beauty,' sighed Herbert. 'Look at the blade.' The postman did a few theoretical swings with it, and then took off his jacket, rolled up his sleeves, and went into action.

Naturally the blacksmith, who came next, admired the new model, and had to satisfy himself by cutting a wide swathe under the trees.

Then Old Nart looked over the hedge and soon had an urge to show what he could do, and once again the rhythmic swish of the scythe was heard in the land, with nothing lacking but home-brewed beer to make it seem like old times.

It brought Sam and Tommy Dodd and Charley Crowe, one after the other, to the busy scene. Nobody could have been more obliging than Herbert in allowing them all to try out the new toy.

'See what you think of it,' he said, and even Old Ben forgot his prejudice against hard graft and had a go.

The tall thistles melted away like wheat before the binder

until only one small clump in the corner remained. 'About time I had a turn,' said Herbert, taking a swing that almost ended up by amputating both his legs.

He is very pleased with the way the new scythe gets the work done.

# Harrowing thoughts

HERE I sit, in the middle of harvest, staring out of my window at the beans on the Dumpling Field and wondering what to write about.

There are the beans, of course. Give 'em beans? Well, it's a crop that always brings memories, not only of bees and blossoms on sunny days, but also of one of my most enlightening experiences in farming many years ago.

At that time I was on a Norfolk farm. They called me a farm pupil, a euphemistic description of an underpaid and overworked farm labourer. On this occasion they had given me two horses to go harrowing beans. The harrows were so heavy that, little as I knew about farming (not much more, in fact, than I know now), it seemed to me that I was murdering the crop.

The old horses trampled it down with their clumsy hoofs, the harrows tore at its roots, and I quite anticipated that the farmer, when he came to view the damage, would have something to say.

☆

HE came just when I was giving the horses (and myself) a bit of a breather on the headlands. Thinking to get one in first, I ventured to say: 'I think we're doin' more harm than good here, boss.'

I shall always remember his reply. 'You do the harrowing,' he said; '*I'll* do the thinking!'

Apparently, like the soldier, I was not being paid to think. But it taught me a lesson—that he was right, and that the more you harrow beans the better they grow. When he walked away I thought how much nicer it would be if somebody else did the harrowing and I could walk about like him and do the thinking. I'm not quite so sure about it now.

For here I sit thinking while Sam is doing the harrowing outside. I can see him on one of the barley stubbles we have just cleared of baled straw. It has been ploughed shallowly, and he is pulling it about with the harrows. Perhaps some of the weed seeds, such as wild oats, will germinate, and we shall be able to destroy them.

If there is anything Sam has a greater contempt for than reading as a waste of time ('reading your senses away,' as he terms it) it is writing or, perhaps I should say, trying to write.

I can see him out there on the stubble, whistling as he rides on his tractor, smiling to himself as the sun shines on him, and no doubt congratulating himself that he is not like some other men. It looks a nice cushy job.

What shall I write about this week? Suddenly I have a harrowing thought, though a happy one. I will go out and yell to him, above the roar of the tractor: 'Come on, you do the thinking, I'll do the harrowing!'

Yes, I think I will.

# Sam gets his dew

BEANS ARE what Sam always calls a 'haz'able' crop.

It means that anything can happen to them and usually does. Occasionally, it is true, we get a bean year, but almost every year we find that the best time to grow them will be next year.

Yet they have their advantages. The sows like them; at

this moment they are acting as gleaners on the bean stubble, mopping up all the shelled-out beans that have been left by the combine-harvester. As a black-straw crop, too, they make a change for the land and a good preparation for the wheat crop that follows. But what I like most about them is that they help us to keep the harvest going smoothly.

On many of these summer mornings, especially before a hot day, you need gumboots when you walk through the fields. There is a heavy dew. We always talk about it as a Rare Old Dag.

☆

SOMEHOW that phrase describes it best. It is like wading through a pond. It makes everything too wet to start harvest operations, with one exception. We can still cut the beans.

We tried cutting ours in the middle of a day of blazing sun. Before the combine had completed the first circular tour of the field, it was obvious we were losing most of the crop. The black pods opened in the heat. The man on the machine shook his head gravely. The beans strewed the stubble.

Sam joined us. He knows how many beans make five, at least so far as any farming problem is concerned. 'Wait till tomorrow morning,' he suggested. 'We may get an old dag.'

Such a morning, of course, would play havoc with harvesting plans for cutting the wheat or the barley or baling up the straw. But it will be just right for the beans. The dew will prevent them from shelling out.

The morning came. I saw Sam bringing old Judy in from the meadow for milking. I had no need to look at his smiling face. His wet feet told me everything I wanted to know.

'It's all right,' says Sam. 'We can cut the old beans this morning. There's a Rare Old Dag.'

# SEPTEMBER

*Harvest over, Sam and Old Nart are watching the new draining machine at work. Pulled by two giant engines it tears a deep trench through two feet of clay and lays the main drain pipes as it moves along.*

*With its help we shall mole-drain four of the wettest fields of the farm.*

*Yesterday when digging we came across an old battered drain pipe of a queer shape lying broken in the clay. The men who put it there, perhaps a hundred years ago (farmers come and go but the land goes on) will surely approve of what we are doing now.*

*Old Nart does. 'Treat this old land like a baby,' he advises Sam. 'Keep its face clean, of course. But also'—he waggles a warning finger—'keep its bottom dry!'*

# Charley sticks to horses

CHARLEY CROWE is one of the last diehard supporters of the horse. He still does all his farming with his old Suffolks. Only once was he persuaded to ride on a tractor. Then he finished up in the ditch, because the only way to stop it he knew anything about was to keep shouting 'Whoa.'

So when, on the other side of the hedge skirting the Dumpling Field, I saw a tractor salesman talking to him the other day I thought that the former might have spent his time as profitably talking to one of my old sows gleaning barley on the stubble. The two of them were obviously engaged in the old tractor-against-horse argument and, to reinforce his side of it, the tractor-man was pointing across the fields, where the tractors and combine-harvesters were busy all round us when I joined them.

Looking back I could see my own little mechanised army advancing over the barley stubble, snorting smoke and fumes. It always impresses me with a sense of the continuing progress of agriculture and of my overdraft. A solemn thought. Ever since the days when old Captain and Honey did most of this work for us, so many mechanical aids have become available that the only question to decide is whether to invest in all of them, or retire on the money.

☆

IT is not only the combine-harvester that has transformed the harvest. The loose straw left behind it is now being gathered up and tightly tied into oblong bales, scattered like a careless child's bricks over the field. It is a hired machine which cost well over a thousand pounds, another small item in the harvest balance sheet.

Now I see Sam, an impressive sight, careering over the stubble on his tractor (the Flying Flea) with a seven-pronged contraption in front for lifting everything by hydraulic power into a tip-up trailer. His only regret is that all these new inventions didn't, as he says, 'come into force' a great many years ago.

But Charley persists in thinking differently. The persuasive salesman is still talking. 'When these tractors are put up in the shed you don't have to feed and look after them,' he says. 'When they're not working you can forget about them.'

Charley looks round at his own stubble where the little pigs are scurrying about and nosing for the new corn. He pats his old horses as they stand champing their bits harnessed to the old binder. He remains unconvinced. 'When my old hosses are working,' he says with a significant glance at the tractors in the next field belching smoke, *'they're not eating!'*

# Bad lot makes good

MY NEIGHBOUR Old Ben has never had a good word to say for his farm. Of course, he could never make it pay. He had to live on his losses. There was the high cost of labour; the crops suffered from every trouble you could imagine, from rust and blight and mildew to wireworms and flea-beetles.

In summer he was plagued with wasps and flies; in winter there was always a morass of mud round the farmhouse, rats came into the kitchen, and rain leaked through the roof. His livestock were a constant menace and worry. Either the cows were in the corn, or the sheep 'blown', or the horses lame, or some old sow or other was always breaking out of her sty and doing untold damage to his or other people's property.

Even worse was the weather down his lane. Snow piled up there deeper than anywhere, the mud was muddier, the wind-frosts were colder, and he was either suffering from too much rain or too little, so that nothing seemed to go right for long.

☆

UNTIL the other day when he decided to retire and sell up.

This was naturally a great occasion, as could be seen by the crowd that, in our market town, flocked into the back room at the Fox & Goose to listen to the auctioneer.

He described the farm at great length. A hundred-odd acres of rich arable land, well-farmed and in good heart, a farmhouse with a wealth of oak beams, a well-built cow-house, and a full complement of farm buildings.

'Now who'll give me just a start at six thousand?' he asked. . . . 'Well then, five . . . or four? Well, gentlemen, start me where you like.'

Somebody ventured a bid of a thousand. 'Ha, ha,' laughed the auctioneer, 'what *part* of the farm do you want?'

Then a voice said two, and another three, and a third four.

It was at this point that the man with the hammer became persuasive. It was productive land, with a good house. I glanced at Old Ben, half-hidden at the back of the room, and wondered whether he was thinking about the snow that came through the roof last winter.

Then the bidding went up in hundreds. 'What's a hundred pounds these days?' asked the auctioneer. He went on: 'You're buying something that won't let you down—in good seasons and bad. A little gold-mine.'

He became confidential. 'I was talking to the owner only this morning. He told me the farm had done him very well all the time he's been there.' I saw Old Ben smile. He smiled more a bit later when the farm had sold for a thousand pounds more than the most he had expected to

136

get for it. No wonder there were warm congratulations from his cronies who now crowded round him, with more than one suggestion about a drink.

The old farm had changed, but not Old Ben. 'Drinks these days are nearly as expensive as farms,' he said.

# His motto—
# 'Don't arger'

'DON'T ARGER,' says the little old man sitting behind his pint pot in the Shepherd & Dog.

'Folks come in here and say this, that and t'other, and whatever it is I always holds with 'em. Then other folks come in and say just the opposite, and I holds with them as well. 'That's my motto,' and he repeats it, wiping his mouth—'Don't arger.'

This is a new philosophy to me, but I can see its advantages. My town friend Herbert, renowned for his eccentric views on everything—religion, politics and farming included—is now in animated conversation with the little man, and presently I see him cheerfully replenishing the pint pot.

I shall have to commend the idea to Sam and Old Nart. Just lately they seem to be arguing about everything. A few days ago it was about the peas and when they would be fit to harvest, and yesterday it was about the red clover and whether we should seed it or cut a second crop for hay, and today it was the potatoes. They were the big old potatoes called Arran Banners. How many tons were there per acre? Old Nart thought eight and Sam said ten. Well, we shall soon know when we plough them out. Or shall we?

☆

IT was a picture of plenty when the plough turned out a mass of potatoes strewn over the black soil. Stooping in the rows and picking them up were the 'good old gals' that Sam had recruited from the village to give us a helping hand.

All went well, with Sam holding on for dear life to the deep-digger plough and hopping over the clods and calling out 'Gertcher' and 'Cubbyeer' to the horses, while the baulks yielded up their rich harvest, and the filled sacks stood up like soldiers paraded in open formation across the field. We should soon know. But Sam, Old Nart and the boy George were still arguing when the sweating horses came back to the stable at noon. How many tons, and how many sacks should we want?

It went on endlessly. It would, I think, be going on now if Herbert hadn't arrived from the pub to switch the debate from potatoes to politics.

Parish politics, in fact. The question—ought we to have a village sign set up on the green, saying Lesser Snoring? Two questions crop up—What do we get out of it? And— Who's going to pay for it?

Incredibly, according to Herbert, the parish council have been told we must pay for the sign ourselves. It will cost a 4*d*. rate. So Old Ben and his cronies are against it. As he points out, we know where we are; we may be a lot of fools but we're not lost.

Sam and I are *for* the sign. We suggest it should be placed opposite the Shepherd & Dog. Then when summer visitors arrive we'll point it out and explain that it has been put there for their benefit.

Results, we hope, will exceed the 4*d*. rate, especially if, like the little man with the pint pot, we 'dont arger'!

# Great expectations

ALL ROUND me the bare golden stubbles tell of harvest gathered in. It is a comforting sight. It reminds me that now is about the right time to go down the lane to the Shepherd & Dog to hear Old Ben's annual commentary.

Take a seat on the oak settle under the smoky oil lamp and listen to the oracle. Everybody looks cheerful and the impression of a harvest-thanksgiving is emphasised by Tommy Dodd's prize marrow on a shelf behind the bar.

We like these visual examples of crop yields. They are more convincing than what Charley Crowe 'laid his barley at,' or Old Nart's estimates of the wheat output.

In the same way we listen respectfully to what Ben has to say, now that harvest is over. There is the evidence of the man on the combine who sacked up the corn. There is the lorryman as witness who carted it away. There is the verdict of the weighing machine in the barn.

The only possible element of doubt, if he happens to mention the round figure of twenty sacks an acre, is about the sizes of his acres.

☆

So we listen to Old Ben, and to the usual digressions, until we come to the harvest.

'It's been a good one,' he declares. 'Some years we get a good corn year, and sometimes a good sugarbeet year. This year we've got both. Except that never before have I seen the old rooks and pigeons do so much damage on the barley and peas.'

'How'd *your* corn come out?' I ask him.

Old Ben reflects long enough for me to remember to stand him a pint. 'Fairly well,' he admits. 'Mind you,' he adds, lifting a finger and summing up his harvest in a single sentence. 'It didn't come out at what I laid it at— *but then I never expected it would.*'

It sums up most of our harvests. We sow the crops, watch them grow, estimate their yields, harvest them, and realise, when they don't come up to expectations, that we never expected they would.

# Old Nart's annual

LET NOBODY say Old Nart is not a devout member of our village society. With unfailing regularity he attends church once a year for the harvest thanksgiving. It is a tribal festival. Everybody is there. From lowly farms and along winding lanes we all converge on a little church so surprisingly crowded that chairs are placed in the aisle and under the gallery.

Old Ben is there, staring round him and nudging his missus. He has to look twice at Sam in new breeches and shiny buskins. There is Mary the land-girl, smart in a special hair-do. Tommy Dodd in a blue suit looks as unfamiliar as Old Nart himself with collar and tie.

We sing 'Plough the Fields and Scatter'. The collection is taken up by our worthy friends the butcher and the postman. And all around us in alcoves and on walls and font are the fruits and flowers of our fields. These are what we have come to see and more particularly to note how prominently or otherwise the ladies of the congregation have placed our own contributions to this festive display.

The marrows are from Tommy Dodd's garden. That sheaf of wheat is from the Dumpling Field. Over there are the boy George's cabbages and Mary's brown eggs and Charley Crowe's apples. That shining heap of potatoes, carefully scrubbed, comes from Old Nart himself.

All of these exhibits are but a small return for the good harvest we have had this year. The huge loaf on the altar is from the baker. Tomatoes and cucumbers from Herbert decorate the base of the pulpit.

AND the preacher. . . . Now here was a man we could understand, who knew something about farming, even though he came from another village. He began: 'I don't know how you've all been getting on, but I expect very much the same as in my village, where we've still got a tidy bit of barley lying about and several haven't finished harvest yet.'

What a sermon it was, and how well the church looked, crowded with so many familiar faces.

Old Nart liked the choir in their new red gowns and surplices, and the girls in their new hats, while Mary enjoyed the congregational singing of the hymns with Charley Crowe chiming in always a few beats behind everybody else. As for Old Ben, what he was looking for was his own record-breaking fodder beet.

There it was, suspended a little precariously over the parson's head. But it stays there through the sermon and while we sing the last hymn and through the benediction. It will stay there over the pulpit until tomorrow afternoon when all these gifts are auctioned in the church porch and Ben will buy it back again. After that it will find its final resting-place as an impressive symbol of a bountiful harvest on the shelf behind the bar at the Shepherd & Dog.

When I got there a bit later, I found everybody talking about the service, the display, the sermon, the singing, the choir, the wonderful congregation, a best-ever harvest thanksgiving. Even Old Nart, sinner though he is, was duly impressed.

'You know,' he said, 'I reckon that old marrow there was the biggest I ever did see!'

# Inside story

ALL THE talk in the Shepherd & Dog is about the latest sensation, the coming of the X-ray survey unit to the village next Saturday.

The 'do', as we call it, takes place in the local school. It is a good move, we agree. Our ex-schoolmaster, Mr Britten, has explained the idea: 'Very much the same as testing the cows for TB,' he tells us. 'There are four new drugs which will cure anybody in the early stages,' he goes on, 'and will certainly stop spread of the infection to others. It could be stamped out altogether if everybody had the test of an X-ray.'

Old Nart—'never had a doctor in seventy years and never ailed anything'—is the one dissentient. 'I've never had an X-ray and I'm not goin' to start now,' he declares.

'I think you'd like it,' says the schoolmaster persuasively.

'I don't want to like it,' says Old Nart, 'and I'm not a-coming.'

142

But the door-to-door canvass, organised by the parson, has been largely successful. There is some doubt about how many will attend, of course. Some of us do not like getting ready and togging up, and having to be somewhere at a fixed time. Others say that they don't want to know what is the matter with them.

But on one thing all of us in Lesser Snoring are agreed.

It is that anyone, or any X-ray unit for that matter, that can manage to see through Old Ben (to say nothing of various other characters in the village) will be doing something that has never been done before.

# The last roll call

MY FARM implements are lined up in long straight rows on the meadow, like decrepit old soldiers on parade. Walking out there, peering closely at them, like an old general inspecting an awkward squad, is Old Nart.

I can imagine what he is thinking. These farm sales are a familiar sight just now. As soon as we get the fall of leaf, somebody in farming is sure to turn over a new leaf, and either to move on—as we are doing—or to give up. But there is more in it than that to Old Nart, as he surveys this parade of farm equipment, numbered in lots and ready for the sale.

That old tumbril, for example, with its broad iron-shod wheels and big ladders, reminds him of the days when he harnessed old Captain into it and loaded it with sheaves during a now-forgotten harvest. That single-furrow horse plough which, if we are lucky, may make a shilling or so, brings back pleasant memories of ploughing the Dumpling Field with Honey and Old Don.

Standing next to it is a somewhat dilapidated horse-rake, now worn and battered, but still with its iron seat that once made it a favourite with many a farmer's boy.

Old Nart stumps past them slowly and sadly. He remembers the old set of seed-harrows. Like him, it was pensioned off years ago, though used lately to hold down the loose thatch on a pig-hut. But how often it was his companion on lonely jobs over wide acres of sown fields. And near it that old binder that always kept breaking down but never failed to finish the job.

☆

THEY all have associations for him. He prods the iron watercart and thinks again of Captain. How the old horse hated to have its clanking noise behind him! They stand there, Old Nart's companions, mustered as for a last roll-call. And presently (next week, to be precise) the hammer will fall on them, as it falls now, at this season of the year, on other faithful servants like them on many farms.

But what great opportunities these sales present!

The chance for some farmers to buy at bargain prices things they will probably never want except to sell again at their own dispersal sales, and the chance for others to get rid of all the rubbish they have accumulated through many farming years, and to begin to accumulate it afresh on another farm.

The chance for me to turn over a new leaf.

What a chance, too, for my neighbour Old Ben. Even Nart smiles when he sees the old sugarbeet lifter. It is one that Ben lent me so many years ago that he has forgotten all about it.

Perhaps next week he may buy it to take home again!